Better than Riches

Better than Riches

Frederick Devereux Pile

The Pentland Press Limited
Edinburgh · Cambridge · Durham

First published in 1992 by
The Pentland Press Ltd.
1 Hutton Close
South Church
Bishop Auckland
Durham

ISBN   1 85821 005 4

Typeset by Elite Typesetting Techniques, Southampton.
Printed and bound by Antony Rowe Ltd., Chippenham.

*To Pam
and to my two daughters,
Fiona and Vanessa*

Acknowledgements

I am deeply grateful to the following:-

Josephine – without whose constant encouragement, and unstinting help and advice the book would never have been written.

Fiona – who has typed, and re-typed, drafts of the book without a complaining word; and who, together with her husband, Mark Towse, has given me much help and advice.

Diana Henstock – who has given me enormous encouragement and countless excellent suggestions, all of which I have incorporated in the book.

Angela Trew – for her enthusiastic encouragement and advice and for all her work in checking proofs.

Vanessa and Ursula – for all their encouragement.

Nigel Inglis-Jones, Esq Q.C. – for reading the draft and for his constructive comments.

David Fletcher, Esq., Librarian, The Tank Museum, Bovington Camp – for his assistance in obtaining photographs.

A. W. Green, Esq. – for kindly lending me a number of original photographs.

*'A good name is to be chosen
rather than great riches.'*

Proverbs 22:1

Contents

Contents

15. The Suez Operation – 1956   69

16. A tour of duty at the Pentagon   76

17. A final tour of duty at the War Office   83

18. Vaux and Associated Breweries   86

19. The Royal Soldiers' Daughters School   93

20. Journalism, charity and village life   97

21. Remarriage   100

22. Conclusion   102

List of Illustrations

Preface

I have written this account for my family and my nearest friends.

A large part of it necessarily relates to the 1939–1945 war – the biggest and most significant event in the lives of most of my generation. However, the way in which any of us react to such major happenings surely depends much on our earlier preparation and training. For a regular soldier, too, there is inevitably at the end of a military career – the step of leaving the sheltered, ordered and disciplined life of the service and of entering civil life. Thus I felt that these two aspects of the life of a soldier, as well as the war itself, should be covered.

Furthermore, I thought it worth including a certain amount about my father and his various relationships because it does throw some light on the motivation and behaviour of some who reach high rank; he retired at the end of the war as a full General. Finally, because I have included my father, I have also included my mother. After all, it was she, together with her parents, who had the major responsibility for the up-bringing of my brother and myself; she and my father virtually separated after the First World War when I was four – and were finally divorced in 1929.

It does not, however, purport to be anything other than a humble story of an ordinary regular soldier (turned jack of a few other trades in later life) who is quite unqualified to pronounce on the great decisions that were made during the war, but who can only report his thoughts and feelings when carrying out the actions which resulted from these decisions. If I have dwelt at too great length on the war it was perhaps because this was an experience which, I am thankful to say, will not be felt by my children, nor I trust, by my grandchildren; it is therefore one which would not be remembered unless committed to paper.

Chapter 1

Early days

The Normandy landing in 1944 produced some of the heaviest fighting seen in the Second World War and the Germans, as they retreated into their own country, fought with particular tenacity. Since they were equipped with tank and anti-tank guns more powerful than our own, they were able to cause us considerable casualties. The brunt of the battle was borne by our armoured units, which led the advance of the Allied Armies from Normandy, through France, Belgium, Holland and into Germany.

The greater the speed of the advance the greater, of course, were the risks; and no one was anxious to take unnecessary chances – thus incurring heavy casualties – if this could possibly be avoided. Yet the advance simply had to be quick, regardless of the consequences to ourselves. As we landed in Normandy the Germans were already launching their V-1 flying bombs from sites in Belgium and Holland; these were directed on London and other population centres in England. By the time we had arrived in Holland, and could deny them the use of these launching sites, they had developed their newest weapon – the V-2; this was a longer range rocket which could be used to bombard London with devastating effect from sites inside Germany. They were also well on their way to producing the atom bomb. So speed was essential, but the cost was heavy; between landing in Normandy and our arrival in the spring of 1945 on the River Elbe, my squadron had lost thirty-five of the original eighty tank crewmen (either killed or wounded) – and more than twenty-five tanks, though the latter were, of course, replaced.

From the point of view of the Army as a whole, the fortunes of one tank squadron were of small significance; but to the squadron leader himself each action is, of course, a matter of overwhelming importance. My life at that time was – singlemindedly – with my squadron. I knew the men intimately; I ate and slept amongst them and I tried to share all their worries. As time goes on in battle one gets more used to death, but it never becomes quite commonplace otherwise we would not revert to our civilised selves after a war is over; but I never got used to the loss of a man in my squadron.

The maintenance of morale is, I believe, only made possible by this enormous comradeship which exists within a unit; whether they are officers, warrant officers, non-commissioned officers or troopers they are your friends – and you simply cannot let your friends down even if you are asked to do the apparently impossible. Though a squadron leader has considerable powers of punishment in wartime, I have no recollection of awarding any punishment or penalty to any man under my command during the campaign – except to send a soldier back and out of the fighting, the most dreaded punishment of all. It was General Horrocks, who commanded the 30 Corps during the Normandy campaign, who described the front line as 'the most exclusive club in the word'; he was right.

Few soldiers – regular or not – can view their first baptism of fire with anything other than apprehension. Apart from the obvious fear of being hit, there is the dreadful worry that one might not be able to rise to the occasion and that one might let down one's comrades; indeed the latter fear is the greatest antidote I know to any risk of failure to do one's duty. It is also difficult for British people to work up hate and to kill, but it has to be done. In one of my first actions in France, I managed, with one other tank, to surprise quite a large force of Germans who then ran for cover into ditches, hedges or just dips in the ground; I could see many of them clearly and they were totally at our mercy, but we were forced to open fire as they had not surrendered. If we had not done so they would soon have re-formed and returned to attack us, possibly at night when we were more vulnerable; but it was difficult.

All this was, I suppose, the acid test of the value of one's early preparation and training – particularly the training which related to development of character and to learning the basis of leadership. Without this my performance would have been worse and my mistakes even more numerous. I had gone to a good preparatory school – Stoke House at Seaford – and, from there to Weymouth College and thence to Sandhurst; from Sandhurst I was commissioned into the Royal Tank Corps (as it then was). One could not expect a very normal education such as this to prepare one for all the demands of war; only battle itself could do this.

The most profound and valuable element of my education was undoubtedly Weymouth. It was a small and less well-known school, yet it had a headmaster, A.G. Pite, who was considered by many to be one of the best in the country; he subsequently went on to become headmaster at Cheltenham but, tragically, died whilst still in his forties. Not only was he a brilliant scholar, whose teaching made some impression even on one so academically unreceptive as myself, but, serving as a prefect under his guidance, with the powers of discipline and punishment normal for prefects in those days, taught me things about leadership, service and moderation (and how closely related these qualities are) which I never forgot.

A very small event is perhaps worth mentioning in view of something that happened twelve years later. In 1932, Mr. Pite arranged for me, at the age of sixteen, to go to France to improve my French, since this was a compulsory subject in the Sandhurst examination. I was placed in the charge of an excellent man called Monsieur Saglio, who lived at Le Mesnil de Breville in Normandy; Breville was a hamlet some ten miles from Caen. Good teacher though he was, a month was really too short a time to learn very much, but I enjoyed this visit as his family were my own age. It was my first experience of getting to know foreigners of any nationality and this was valuable. I also got to know the area well. As I shall tell later, I returned to this scene in 1944.

Chapter 2

With Bam and Jock in London

In 1929, after her divorce, my mother (always known as Bam) married Jock Ferguson – then a Major in the Durham Light Infantry. After the marriage they went to Catterick where the regiment was stationed. In 1933 Jock was asked by Lord Trenchard if he would transfer to the Metropolitan Police, which at that time was going through a thorough reorganisation. After a lot of thought, and bearing in mind that he had just become a father (Iain was born in 1932) and that the Police would give him a longer career than the Army, he agreed to transfer. He was given an appointment at Scotland Yard and they moved to London, taking a maisonette at 33 Cleveland Square, Bayswater. I spent much time with them in London and it was from their house that I took the Sandhurst entrance exam in November 1933 at the age of seventeen; and, having passed this (just), that I went off to Sandhurst two months later to start the course. After three years at Scotland Yard, Jock became the commandant (one of the last) of the Hendon Police College, which produced so many excellent chief constables for forces all over the country in the 1950s and 1960s. He later became Chief Constable, first of Sussex, where he amalgamated the East and West Sussex Police into one force, and then of Kent.

Both my mother and Jock were a tower of strength to me. She was totally unselfish, full of common sense and understanding and had a marvellous sense of humour. She was, until her last day, a most courageous person. It is interesting, though perhaps not strictly relevant to this account, that though she was through her life very poor she always managed to dress superbly and entertain generously – matters to which she attached much importance. I believe that few people knew how poor she was. She took an infinite interest in her family and, in particular, her grandchildren.

It was because of her that the fact that I had come from a broken home assumed no significance for me whatever; nor did I at any stage feel in the least deprived.

From schooldays Jock had much influence over me and had, in many ways taken the place of my father; he was always a great encouragement to me. When I went to Sandhurst he took his usual interest; he had been a good horseman himself and he did all he could to help me ride well. This was a compulsory subject at that time at Sandhurst and one to which the authorities attached much (some might now say too much) significance. I had shown some promise over this. Indeed I hoped (and half expected) to be chosen to ride for the 'Saddle' – the highest riding award at Sandhurst; the winner being regarded as second only to the cadet who received the Sword of Honour. My prowess in this respect was, however, to be short-lived and I feel that I must relate an anecdote which, for ridiculous folly and conceit, would be hard to beat; nevertheless, I believe it to be unique.

I used always to go to Cleveland Square for my 'leaves' as my father was in Egypt. On one such occasion, in order to keep my hand in with the riding, Jock arranged with the Adjutant of the Royal Horse Guards at Knightsbridge Barracks, Captain (later General) Laycock, for me to ride one of their horses each morning. Jock himself rode a police horse every day; indeed this, more often or not, was his method of transportation to Scotland Yard from Cleveland Square. So we arranged to meet in Hyde Park, not far from the bridge over the Serpentine. The first day I collected the animal I had been allocated (which seemed to me inordinately large) and crossed over the road from the barracks into Rotten Row. Having got thus far without incident the horse, clearly dissatisfied with his rider, raised himself on his hind legs and it was not long before he had me in a state of acute concern. At this moment he decided to bolt and bolt he did; we rapidly got going westward, towards the Serpentine, and reached the point where I had arranged to meet Jock but – alas – at full gallop. Only for one moment did I have any say about our progress, or our route; that was the point at which the bridge and the Row meet. Here the animal hesitated for a second and I was able to persuade him to take the left fork – thus remaining in the Row – rather than crossing the bridge on which the inevitable emergency landing would clearly have been more painful.

As we completed a full circle of the Row and again appeared opposite Knightsbridge Barracks the horse, without warning, crossed the road, aiming for the barrack gate. However, so fast was he going, that in weaving between the cars he missed the gate by about five yards and we found ourselves galloping down the pavement towards the Albert Gate. Here there were two lines of stationary traffic held up by the traffic lights; at this point a kind mounted policeman, who had earlier spotted my dilemma, put his horse between mine and the cars. The two horses collided and fell; and I slid gently over the roofs of two cars and landed unhurt on the ground. I am very glad to say that neither of the horses suffered any damage either. I returned to Bayswater on a bicycle, and gave up forever any illusion that I could ride a horse.

As I have said, the incident may have been unique, but it was no subject for pride.

Chapter 3

Joining the Army

I joined the Army – The Royal Tank Corps – in August 1935 at Bovington Camp, Dorset. This had been my father's regiment since, though a 'gunner' in the First World War, he transferred in 1922 to the newly-formed R.T.C. In those days it would have seemed quite unnatural for a young cadet at Sandhurst not to follow in a soldier-father's footsteps.

All newly joined young officers spent six months at Bovington Camp for courses in tank driving and maintenance and wireless, and to learn something about the Regiment. This was followed by a further three months training in gunnery at the sister school at Lulworth Camp. Not only was this our first indication of what life in a tank would be like, but it was our first experience of an officer's mess. My pay was 10/– (50p in to-day's terms) a day, and my mess bill was seldom less than £13 a month; so it was difficult to make ends meet financially. I was lucky in that, for a few years, I had an allowance of £100 a year from my father; though this advantage was a bit reduced as he had insisted that I should keep a horse. Not only was this expensive but it was also time consuming; and I was not, at this stage, so very interested in horses. However, I did manage, aided by the small mechanical knowledge I was acquiring, to run a very old car as well.

Not that any of us had much time to drive about in a car (nor, for that matter, to ride a horse). Our courses kept us busy till late afternoon and there was a good deal of preparation for the following day's training; furthermore, we were required to dine in the mess (in mess kit) three times a week. We were also obliged to 'call' on every married officer; this involved arriving at the house between 4.00 p.m. and 6.00 p.m. for a short visit. If the officer and his wife were out, we left two engraved visiting cards (one for the officer and one for his wife). In due course one would be asked back for tea or perhaps (and better) a drink. Since there were about forty married officers this whole process took much time, and it was not very exciting for either party!

7

The Royal Tank Corps was at that time probably better trained for war than any other formation of the British Army; but it was poorly equipped. It consisted of eight battalions of Vickers Medium and Light tanks which had been manufactured just after the 1914–1918 War and were totally out of date. Four of these battalions formed the Tank Brigade and were assembled at Tilshead on Salisbury Plain for three months' hard training each summer, supervised by its commander Brigadier (later Major General Sir Percy) Hobart. As a consequence of this training the Tank Brigade – the only one in the Army – had, by 1937, achieved a high degree of efficiency despite its out-of-date equipment. As 1939 (and war) drew closer it increasingly received the attention both of politicians and (reluctantly) of the Army's senior officers. During the years before the outbreak of war, the number of our tank units was greatly increased, and the Royal Armoured Corps came into being; this consisted of the eight units of the Royal Tank Corps – now to be renamed the Royal Tank Regiments – and the Cavalry Regiments. Some of the latter had already been mechanised; those still equipped with horses were instructed to retrain as armoured regiments without delay.

The Tank Brigade became the nucleus of our first armoured division. Eventually, in the war, the Royal Armoured Corps comprised eighty-four armoured or armoured car regiments, eleven training regiments, numerous ancillary and specialised units together with vastly enlarged schools at Bovington and Lulworth. This reorganisation and expansion placed an enormous strain on the Royal Tank Regiment (and its well-trained Territorial Army associated units), who had not only to raise and train more units themselves but also to provide instructors for mechanising cavalry regiments; it was also required to produce most of the instructors needed for the newly formed training regiments.

In 1936, during my first summer training season on Salisbury Plain, an incident occurred which very nearly ended my military career almost before it had begun. I was taking a turn at umpiring another battalion's exercise: this involved sitting on the outside of the troop-leader's tank, on a ledge just above the driver. From this position it was possible to shout to the troop-leader above the noise of the tank's engine – and he to me. It was also possible to hear the radio and make written notes which were essential to the 'post mortem' after the exercise. The tank driver normally drove with his armour-plated visor locked back so that he had a wide view of the ground to his front; the umpires (including myself) used this visor to hang on to when the tank was rocking about over rough country. The tank on which I was travelling was moving fast for those days (about twenty m.p.h.) with its gun turned broadside to engage an imaginary enemy; unfortunately, before I could see what was happening, its commander allowed it to go too near a tree which caught the gun as we passed. This caused the turret to revolve rapidly, pinning me between the sharp corner of a protruding armoured 'bulge' (which housed the radio set) at its rear and the visor onto which I was holding.

I was taken to hospital at Tidworth and, after a few days, discharged on sick leave to recuperate. I spent this period with my grandparents at Hove; whilst there I suddenly became very ill and had to have an emergency operation, followed by a long convalescence of about four months.

All this did, of course, set back my training a good deal. There had, however, been one cheerful event a few weeks earlier that summer. In the middle of the training period we were allowed a fortnight's break and I also spent this with my grandparents. I should perhaps add at this point that, due to my not having a proper home during the greater part of my schooldays and to my mother's poverty, my brother John and I were virtually brought up in Hove by our grandparents; thus it seemed quite natural to regard them as 'home'. Also here at the time of my leave were the Henstock family who lived in Newbury (where I had an uncle who introduced me) but who took their grandparents' Hove house, called 'Quietways', each summer. I met the family and liked them enormously; indeed, I saw a lot of them during this fortnight and, within a few months, was engaged to the eldest girl – Pamela. She was then twenty-three; her younger sisters – Cynthia and Diana – were eighteen and sixteen respectively.

Having very little to do during my convalescence I took a course in 'Pelmanism' – and a very valuable training it was. One question to which the instructors repeatedly returned was 'What are your main objects in life?' I had to think hard and long about it as it was not something I was conscious of being bothered with at this stage. Certainly my main objects had nothing to do with ambition – I had seen how much harm this could do in my father's case. Finally I gave my reply as two aims. Firstly to do every job or duty that came to hand as well as I could without requiring praise, approval or reward; and secondly to have a happy marriage and family. The first (rather lofty) aim was one I have all too often failed to attain, but it has always been there nevertheless as a challenge; I can only think I put the second one down as a result of my parents' experience. I do not think I have ever wanted to change these, though I might have gone to greater heights in the Army if ambition had figured a little larger.

I had done badly at Sandhurst (passing in very low and out even lower) and as a result, when in January 1937 I was sent on my first really big course, no one in the Regiment expected very much from me; it was a six-month course held at the Military College of Science at Woolwich. Since my mother and stepfather then lived in London I thought that the course would suit me admirably, as I could go home at frequent intervals and fully intended to do so. In addition Pam had started a course in flower arranging in London and I was often able to get away to have lunch with her. One evening, at his house in Cleveland Square, Jock started submitting me to some searching questions regarding my progress on the Woolwich course – and he was highly dissatisfied with my answers. He made it clear to me that I should spend more time at my work and less at home – and far less with my girl friend; he added that, contrary to what anyone else might think of my prospects, he himself expected me to achieve a really good result.

So I started to do a good deal more work; I had to as I was not welcomed home! As the weeks went by I found the work a bit easier and seemed to be getting things right more often; and when the final results came out at the end of the course I found, to my amazement, that I had passed out top.

I went, after the course had ended, to stay at Cleveland Square with my mother and Jock who seemed very pleased with what had happened. Some months later he quietly produced and gave me a small parcel. It contained a silver cigarette case engraved with my name and the words, 'Woolwich 1937'. He was far from being a rich man; and in many ways he was a difficult man. However, what he did for my self-confidence at this period would be difficult to overstate; for me it was a turning point.

Not only were my mother and Jock of great help in the various ways I have described but they were – particularly after my Woolwich course – very understanding of my engagement to Pam. I was only twenty-one which, in those days, was considered too young; but they both made it quite clear to Pam that she was welcome to stay with them at Cleveland Square whenever she wanted to. This was important to me as my father was totally against it and even wrote to my prospective father-in-law pointing out what a poor prospect I was. This letter, I must add, completely misfired; Philip Henstock could not have been kinder to me from the moment I met him.

My mother and Jock used to go on holiday for a fortnight each summer to the Belgian resort of Le Zoute; this was a splendid seaside place for Iain, their young son, and countless other young children. It also had a golf course and an excellent casino and dance hall which were of more interest to their elders. In 1938, just before I was due to go out to Egypt, they asked me to come and stay – at their expense – at their small hotel in Le Zoute, and to bring Pam with me. This I did and we had a delightful holiday. It was a particularly pleasant break from thoughts of Egypt, war and the very uncertain future which faced all of us.

Chapter 4

Training for war

I sailed for Egypt in the late summer of 1938 when war with Germany was
starting to look almost certain. I joined the 6th Royal Tank Regiment in
Abbassia – between Cairo and Heliopolis (so large has Cairo now become
that the two towns are virtually indistinguishable). General Hobart (Hobo)
had come out at about the same time with a small staff, to form the 7th
Armoured Division. This new division embraced the 1st and 6th Royal
Tank Regiments together with the 7th and the 8th Hussars; there was also a
battalion of the Rifle Brigade and a regiment of the Royal Artillery. This
division comprised virtually the whole of our ground attacking strength in
Egypt at that time.

Before Hobo arrived in Egypt the working day started early, but it
stopped at midday when those who wished to do so played tennis at the
Gezira Club, polo, or some other sport. In the evening officers would quite
often go to the club swimming pool to bathe, followed by a whisky and soda
or two by the water's edge. Practically no one worked during the afternoon.
By the time Hobo had got settled in – about a week after he had arrived –
all this was stopped; we continued to start work early, as is necessary in all
hot countries, but our duties now carried on all day and well into the
evening whilst we were in Cairo. Increasingly, however, we were not in
Cairo but in the desert, learning to navigate and generally accustoming
ourselves to this life. 'A war is coming,' Hobo told us in one of his early
talks, and 'we must be prepared for it; this means first class training and no
excuse acceptable for failure; nothing short of excellence will be good
enough.' Furthermore, he made it clear that our relatively comfortable life
in Cairo was to come to an end in days rather than months and that,
henceforward, we would mostly live and work in the desert near Sollum on
the Libyan frontier, so that we really knew the area.

In the 6th Royal Tanks I had, for the first time, some real, unsupervised

11

military responsibility. I was placed in command of a section of five light tanks; these were intended for reconnaissance, and a thorough knowledge of the desert was even more essential for us than for the medium tank sections which did not range so far afield. We were therefore encouraged to take our sections out into the desert on our own for several days at a time. This involved learning – fast – the principles of administration. Everything had to be taken with us – rations, water, petrol, essential spare parts and the means of repairing or recovering our tanks if they broke down or got stuck. It was all admirable training for a young officer.

Back in Abbassia I had as a squadron leader an excellent chap called 'Tiger' Lyons. He was far senior to me – about forty years old – and had an appalling temper, particularly when he met anything smacking of humbug; but he had a heart of gold and we all regarded him with great affection. Sadly he died as a prisoner of war after he returned to Europe in the early part of 1940, after playing a most gallant part in the defence of Calais during the Army's withdrawal to Dunkirk.

Tiger left us alone to run our sections without obvious supervision. We planned our tactical exercises in the desert, we looked after the mechanical efficiency of our tanks and their equipment but, above all, we learned to look after our men – their training and every aspect of their well being. Periodically there would be a conference to consider promotions within the squadron; Tiger would then have in all the section commanders, together with the Squadron Sergeant Major. He would announce the vacancies that were available and would ask each of us for our recommendations; on one such occasion he said that there were two vacancies for promotion to sergeant and that he considered that one of these should go to my section as I had, for some time, been one short – 'Who did I suggest?' he asked. I said that I felt that a Corporal Manthorpe should be promoted. 'Oh,' he said, 'but why did you not propose Corporal Morris?' Now Corporal Morris was a splendid non-commissioned officer – one of the best in many respects, full of character, experienced and well liked by all those who served under him; he had, however, recently got himself into some minor trouble in Cairo for which he had been reprimanded. So, thinking that Tiger would blow me through the roof for suggesting him, I decided it would be better to play safe. Tiger simply bristled with fury. 'What business is it of yours whether I agree with you or not?' he thundered; 'you have really got to have confidence in your own judgment and, if I do not agree with you, you must have the guts to stick to your guns and try to persuade me.'

He repeated his original question, and I rather lamely said what, in my heart, I had wanted to in the first place – that I recommended Corporal

Morris in the confidence that he had now learned his lesson. Tiger at once agreed, and Corporal Morris became Sergeant Morris, and was placed in command of two light tanks. As I left the office at the end of the meeting Tiger stopped me and said, 'You have learned a lesson too, and I know you are going to do well.' He was never a man to bear a grudge and, a few weeks later, he saw that Corporal Manthorpe was promoted too.

In two years Morris had so proved himself in the desert battles that, by the end of 1940, he had been commissioned; and, by the end of 1942, he was a major with a Military Cross. Sadly he was killed whilst still in the Middle East and I never saw him again.

By the time war broke out on 3rd September 1939, Hobo had achieved a complete transformation of the training and efficiency of the units under his command; he had, however, also become very unpopular with those senior to him. In particular, General Gordon-Finlayson, the Commander of British Troops in Egypt, did not approve of these 'new' ideas nor of Hobo's singleness of purpose which was so reshaping the lives of all who were serving in Egypt. Initially, too, both the Cavalry and the regiments of the Royal Horses Artillery in his division distrusted him – but not for long.

Late in 1939 Hobo was sacked; shortly afterwards the Division returned to Cairo for a short period of re-fitting and training – and we all heard the news. It went through the Division like wildfire and practically every officer and soldier was appalled at what had been done. I myself went round to his flat on Gezira Island and he received me (a subaltern) as if I myself were a general, though he was close to tears. He made me sit down and have a cup of tea with his wife and himself and, as I left he said, 'Please do not worry about me – just you yourself remember that, if one does not occasionally make enemies in life, one will never get anything worthwhile done.' They both left the following day and, as they drove to Cairo station, the whole route from their flat was lined with cheering soldiers; in particular evidence were large numbers of officers and men from the very regiments which had criticised him earlier, but who now held him in enormous esteem. He returned to England and, as he was not offered another job, immediately enlisted in the Home Guard where he became a corporal. Fortunately Winston Churchill spotted him a year or two later and at once had him reinstated in command of another armoured division – the 11th; he subsequently also raised the 79th Armoured division. The three divisions he had trained had first class fighting records and were widely acclaimed as the best in the Royal Armoured Corps.

A small facet of Hobo's leadership qualities and methods – and one not always recognised since his social life was so subordinated to military needs – was that he was extremely good at a cocktail party. This was one of the chief forms of entertainment amongst officers in Cairo in those days. Over and over again I noticed that he would make a point of speaking to every single person present, and would make each feel that he really mattered. I am sure he learned a lot about the officers he commanded – and their wives – from these conversations; they certainly made a deep and favourable impression on those to whom he spoke.

In November of 1939, after the Regiment had completed its allotted period in Cairo, we again returned to the desert. A curious and comparatively rare occurrence took place soon after we had established ourselves near Mersa Matruh. There was a heavy storm accompanied by torrential rain, so heavy that all the wadis were flooded – and remained flooded for two days. Movement became extremely difficult and the unpleasantness of the situation was aggravated by a plague of scorpions which seemed to regard our beds (in the open by our tanks) as a legitimate refuge!

By March 1940 all the enemy pressure was starting to build up against the British Expeditionary Force in France and the French armies, and there seemed at the time little reason to fear for the defence of Egypt. The Territorial Army had been doubled in strength a year earlier and, at a stroke, every regiment became two; as a result there was an appalling shortage of trained men. Furthermore, soon after war broke out, most of the 'first line' (original) T.A. units had gone to France with the B.E.F. leaving their second-line newly formed units to train as well as they could. However, as the threat to our position in France could be seen clearly, these second-line units were also desperately needed out there. The Army in Egypt was therefore called upon to send home some thirty officers to join these very inexperienced and ill-prepared units, and to go with them to France.

My commanding officer sent for me about this time, when we were still in the desert; he told me the background to the situation in France and said that, as I was engaged to be married, he was going to suggest to the Brigadier that I should be one of the officers to return – albeit briefly – to England. In a few days I was on my way by sea to my new Regiment, the 2nd East Riding Yeomanry.

Pam and I got married on 6th March 1940, two days after I had landed in Southampton; I reported to the 2nd E.R.Y. two days later at Tidworth. We were told that we had a month to get ready and that we would then sail for France.

It was, however, increasingly clear as the days went by that the Regiment (and doubtless other second-line regiments) was totally untrained and that very little had been done to put this right in the year since they had been formed. They had not even got enough competent drivers to take all their vehicles (small Bren gun carriers) out of barracks, and certainly nowhere near enough wireless operators or gunners. Thus, even assuming that drivers could be trained quite quickly up to a tolerable standard, the Regiment would be impossible to control without adequate wireless operators. In addition of course, without trained gunners, the Regiment would be of little use even if we got it to the theatre of war. One's mind boggled at the prospect of our being re-equipped with tanks, though it was certainly the intention that this should happen as and when the tanks became available.

I was promoted Captain after a few days and appointed Technical Adjutant; I was given the duty of training the Regiment so that every vehicle had a proper crew. In order to do this I worked nearly all hours of the day and night getting the more promising N.C.O.s, men – and officers too – on courses. As soon as enough crewmen could be put together to form a troop, I helped the squadron concerned to run exercises to train them in communications and command – so that they, in their turn, could train others; but it was an uphill struggle and, by May 1940 when France fell, we were still hopelessly inefficient.

The depleted remnants of the 1st East Riding Yeomanry, who had fought well but sustained very heavy casualties in France, were evacuated through Dunkirk; they then joined us in Tidworth. Some weeks later the two were amalgamated again into one Regiment; luckily it was to be four years before they would see a shot fired and, by that time, they had become a good Regiment.

In September 1940 I left this Regiment and was sent as an instructor to the 103rd Officer Cadet Training Unit which was then forming in Lanark; it subsequently moved to Perham Down, near Tidworth. In the summer of 1941 I was sent to the Staff College at Camberley, as a student; it was during my course at Camberley that my elder daughter, Fiona, was born – in October 1941, at Newbury. I managed to pass the course and, at the end of it, was promoted to Major and posted to the School of Artillery at Larkhill as the Royal Armoured Corps Instructor; this appointment lasted nine months and, in December 1942, I returned to the Staff College – this time as an instructor.

The work of instructing at Camberley was very demanding as the courses were – rightly – intensive, and preparation by the instructors had to be extremely thorough. We started work at about 8.00 a.m. and rarely got to bed before 2.00 a.m., having prepared the following day's tuition; weekends were almost as busy. Fortunately, thanks to the kindness of a Brigadier 'Buggins' Brunker and his wife Amelia, who were very old friends of my mother, Pam was able to join me for four months as they lent us their house in Camberley. It was the first time we had been together since leaving the 103rd OCTU eighteen months earlier.

In September 1943, just before the end of my last course as an instructor at Camberley, I suddenly became very ill with a recurrence of my abdominal trouble; I was taken to the Cambridge Hospital, Aldershot, and had an operation the same day. I was in hospital (incidentally in the next room to General Horrocks, of whom I saw a great deal during this period, and who had had an almost identical operation) for about six weeks; I was discharged on sick leave at the end of October. Since I was now medically downgraded I could not join my Regiment, which I had set my heart on doing; I was sent temporarily to a staff appointment at Headquarters Eastern Command at Luton Hoo in Hertfordshire. Here I had the galling task of assisting regiments of the Royal Armoured Corps prepare for the landing in France which everyone knew must come soon; I could only hope that I would be considered fit enough to join one of them before it was too late. I had several medical boards but could not persuade the medical authorities to upgrade me until May 1944 – and then only sufficiently to permit me to take a rather inactive staff appointment as a G.S.O.2 (Second Grade Staff Officer) HQ 2nd British Army for the landing; it was located in one of the large forts on the hill overlooking Fareham.

It was here that I was informed of the plan for the landing in Normandy – and promptly told that, now that I knew, I would not be allowed to leave the immediate Headquarters area or telephone to anyone outside it. I was one of six officers who manned a continuous radio watch and who were responsible for keeping the Army Commander (General Dempsey) informed, and the operations map up to date, on a minute to minute basis. We also, of course, covered the actual landing itself on 6th June 1944.

The battle began in the very early hours, with the U.S. and British Airborne landings; followed by Commando landings and the main Seaborne assault at dawn.

Chapter 5

The landing in Normandy

The Tactical Headquarters of 2nd Army (General Dempsey himself and about ten officers) landed on 7th June in the evening and, a few days later, the Chief of Staff (Major General Maurice Chilton) sent for me and told me that he was leaving to join the Army Commander in two hours time and that he wished me to accompany him. We were to cross on a destroyer. It was quite usual in wartime to be told to pack up everything one possessed at very short notice, and I was not therefore surprised at these instructions. On this occasion, however, I took particular care as it was going to be my first experience of battle at close quarters. Small things can be important; I had been given a superb pair of ivory hairbrushes by my mother for my twenty-first birthday and I debated hard in my mind whether to take these with me or not. I decided to do so on the basis that they were there to be used and I might as well have them with me regardless of the risk. Countless soldiers must have agonised over such apparently small matters throughout military history; sadly, I later lost one of the pair (which by that time I was carrying in my bedding roll on the back of my tank) during the breakout from Normandy.

The destroyer docked in the small fishing port of Courseulles, on the Canadian Corps front, and tied up without difficulty at the quayside in the middle of the port. There was desultory shelling in the area but nothing very heavy; and we set out in a jeep for Creuilly, not far from Bayeux, which was to be the Army HQ. Bayeux, incidentally, had been captured on D-Day without sustaining any damage whatsoever, but this was certainly not true of the area around the town. My chief recollection of that drive from Courseulles was the utter destruction of every building *en route*; villages so flattened that you could not see where the roads were meant to go; there were numbers of dead cattle in every field, the consequent nauseating smell of which permeated the atmosphere for miles around. There were also a great number of vehicles, both German and our own, which had been destroyed in the fighting and which had simply been pushed into the side of the road; and, from time to time one came across groups of dead enemy soldiers.

A day or so later, when I was getting ready for a bit of sleep (I had learned rapidly that no good soldier should miss any such opportunity), a messenger appeared and said that the Colonel, General Staff (Selwyn Lloyd, who later became Foreign Secretary), wanted to see me. He told me that I was to leave at once with the Chief of Staff, to find a way round Caen – then the scene of some of the heaviest fighting of the battle – and over a River Orne bridge near the town; and to get him safely to the Headquarters of the 6th Airborne Division commanded by General Gale. The objective of this Division had been to secure the crossings over the River Orne and thus to protect the left flank of the Army. To assist with this there had been heavy bombing by the R.A.F. and most bridges (or the approaches to them) had been rendered impassable.

We set off in a jeep, driving through villages which were nothing more than piles of rubble. There were no signposts and it was often virtually impossible to ascertain where the roads had been, we simply had to guess. Eventually, with some difficulty as map reading was not my strongest point, we found a bridge over the river; beyond it was the small village of Breville in which I was relieved to see a sign pointing to the Airborne Divisional Headquarters. By an amazing coincidence it was in the very same house in which I had spent a month – twelve years earlier – endeavouring to learn French; it had been hit by a German artillery concentration and there was not much of it left.

By this time the Army had, as far as I can remember, been ashore for about ten days and, at the morning staff meetings which I always attended, I continually heard reference to the difficulty we were having in getting a sufficient tonnage of stores ashore to maintain it. This supply was entirely dependent on the 'Mulberry harbours'. These were artificial harbours, manufactured in England and towed across the Channel. They consisted of concrete blocks which formed the breakwater and pierheads which slid up and down with the tide; these were linked to the shore by pontoons. On arrival at Arromanches the concrete blocks of the British Mulberry were sunk correctly and the remainder of the harbour was completed; it was taken into use immediately. The United States Mulberry was also completed at Omaha Beach, but it was later irreparably damaged in a gale.

As we drove back after visiting the Airborne Divisional Headquarters I asked General Chilton about the supply situation which seemed to be causing so much concern; he replied with considerable gravity, 'Make no mistake, Freddy, it really is bloody serious; we are only hanging on by a thread until we can get Cherbourg opened.' The British 'harbour' handled millions of tons of stores for both armies, and without it our situation would have been perilous indeed.

Towards the end of June 1944 a report came into Army HQ that the Commander of the 8th Armoured Brigade (Brigadier Bernard Cracroft of my Regiment) and his Brigade Major had been wounded, the latter being evacuated; the Brigadier's wound was not thought to be serious. A replacement Brigade Major was understood to have been sent for from England but, pending his arrival, I was sent up to fill the appointment.

It was a marvellous opportunity and challenge for me, but I was under no illusion as to the difficulties I would have to face. A Brigade Major in battle does not have an easy job. The Brigade is controlled from a 'command tank' (a tank – in our case a Sherman – which has had its main armament removed to make more room) which had been fitted with two large wireless sets and a large battle map, and clipboards with numerous code names and radio call signs. In the turret would travel the Brigade Commander (unless he was forward visiting one of the Regiments in action), the Brigade Major and the Intelligence (or perhaps Signals) Officer; there was little room to spare. The Brigade Commander would be away for much of the time; He normally then travelled in one of the scout cars (small armoured cars armed with a machine gun only, but containing a wireless set enabling him to keep in constant touch both with his Headquarters and with the regiments under his command; they were known as 'dingoes'). This arrangement, excellent from the point of view of a commander (and incidentally for the availability of space in the command tank) did, however, present problems to his long-suffering staff who had to keep themselves 'in the picture' as to what was being said by – and to – the Commander. The B.M. and his staff officer spent long periods in the tank, receiving radio messages from the regiments and attached units of the Brigade; and receiving information from the Divisional Headquarters as to the situation on our flanks, and also anything that was known from intelligence sources of enemy dispositions. All this would be noted on a clipboard and the battle map kept up to date with the exact location and movements of our own units, neighbouring units and the enemy. Thus the Brigade Commander could see at a glance, as soon as he returned to his tank, how the Brigade was disposed and the relationship of our units to those on our flanks. In addition to the recording of information the B.M. would transmit the Brigade Commander's orders by radio; often these would have to take the form of advice to a regiment as to how to deal with a difficult situation. There would also be a continuous series of instructions and requests for information from the divisional headquarters with whom we were working at the time. All this could well be happening whilst the tank was under shellfire, thus adding to the noise and potential confusion; so it was certainly no place for a quiet life.

At such a moment the proper Brigade Major appeared – Jack Greenwood, of my Regiment, whom I had known as an old friend for many years; he had returned from Egypt in 1940, as I did, and had also gone to a recently formed regiment. Since I last saw him, however, he had spent eighteen months in New Zealand and then a year at the War Office and he did not even have the advantages I had had – of taking part in all the big exercises which occured in England as preparation for the landing in France. Thus it was unfortunate, and very unkind to him, to thrust Jack into a command tank in battle with so little experience. Inevitably he got into difficulties and was sacked. I again found myself in his place.

We came out of the action after I had been with the Brigade for about ten days and, regrettably, during this short period of rest Brigadier Cracroft suffered a complication from his previous wound; this time he had to be evacuated. His place was taken by Brigadier Errol Prior-Palmer, whose previous brigade had been disbanded after the landing; he was a great disappointment after his predecessor. Among other idiosyncrasies, he carried with him a slab of armour plate, which he instructed his batman to place over the slit trench in which he slept every night – surely a bad example for any commander to set when we were sustaining many casualties from enemy shell fire; but he clearly thought he was too valuable to risk. He seemed far more preoccupied with the painting of signs indicating the whereabouts of Brigade HQ than with efficiency or morale. He was as excitable as Brigadier Cracroft had been cool, and the command tank became pandemonium at times as a result. He had, from the start, wanted his previous Brigade Major and he soon had the opportunity he had hoped for, as relations between us got worse every day. After a fortnight with him he gave me the sack.

It was now, as far as I can recall, the last week in July; temporarily unemployed, I went to see the chief administrative officer at HQ 30 Corps, Brigadier George Webb, who happened to be an old friend. He asked me what I wanted to do, and I told him that now that I was fit enough I would like to go to my regiment; he said, 'How about the 1st Tanks?' This suited me well except that, since Jack Greenwood had just gone there, I feared that all the fighting command appointments would be filled. However, he told me that Jack had taken over the Regiment's administrative echelon, and that the Regiment did need a new fighting squadron leader.

So I paddled off in a jeep to join the 1st, now near Falaise, just south of Caen. I had known the commanding officer, Lt. Colonel (later Major General) P.R.C. (Pat) Hobart, D.S.O., O.B.E., M.C., well in years gone by and it was good to see him again; after a few days he offered me 'A' Squadron and indicated that he expected me to ginger it up a bit. Shortly after I arrived another old friend, Major J. J. (Johnny) Dingwall, D.S.O., became the Regimental second-in-command; he had previously been in command of a squadron, and had fought an intrepid action to assist in the capture of Lisieux. It was of inestimable support to the three fighting squadron leaders, during the battles to come, to have two officers with such experience and commonsense in command.

Chapter 6

The advance through Northern Europe

Though Caen had been captured on 9th July 1944, after some very heavy fighting, the area around it was not cleared of Germans until the 5th August. At this time too the U.S. Army had broken through the German defences at St Lo, some thirty-five miles to the west, and were then in a position (with the French 2nd Armoured Division) to advance south and east. It was not, however, until the 19th of August that the wide encircling movement that followed was completed; the U.S. Army, at Chambois, just south-east of Falaise, trapping the German troops that remained in Normandy. After this the way was clear for the general advance to the River Seine and beyond. Paris was captured on 26th August, and the armoured spearheads of the Allied Armies crossed the river soon afterwards.

Then followed an advance on a very broad front. The leading armoured units continually met German detachments which delayed them, but the Germans were unable to form a comprehensive defensive position and thus, as one of our formations was temporarily held up, others advanced unimpeded; consequently the advance as a whole was never seriously delayed. By the 2nd of September, when the advance approached the Belgian Frontier, the 1st Royal Tanks found themselves at Arras; at this point they were allowed forty-eight hours to re-fuel and maintain their tanks. By this time German resistance was building up extensively; the following day the Regiment was ordered to attack and capture the small town of Lillers, not far from Arras, which was believed to be held quite strongly by the enemy.

My squadron were allotted the southern part of the town as our objective, and I was given a platoon of the Rifle Brigade to help with the clearing of houses; It was my first experience of clearing a town, albeit a small one, and I had the feeling that there were Germans popping up everywhere. We seemed much too 'thin on the ground' to deal with them all. However, bit

22

by bit, we moved closer to the centre of the place and, by nightfall, the enemy seemed to have evacuated it; there was, however, a lot of movement in the buildings and hedgerows just outside and every tank (including my own) was needed to guard the approaches in case the enemy counter-attacked and came back. There was no sleep for anyone that night; all had to be fully alert or we would have been an easy target for enemy bazookas (called by the Germans '*Panzerfaust*') – they were short-range, hand-held weapons which fired a shell of enormous power; a direct hit on tank almost invariably knocked it out or at least killed a member of the crew). By the time we were withdrawn, in the early hours of the morning, we had killed or captured some eighty Germans and had taken possession of a considerable number of guns, pistols, cars and much other enemy equipment.

The following day we were sent with orders to capture some high ground overlooking the town of Bethune, which our infantry were having difficulty in clearing. After meeting some opposition – mostly small arms and mortaring, but there was also some anti-tank fire – we arrived at our objective without, I thought, too much trouble. This was, however, a much too complacent thought; I, taking another tank with me, decided to drive forward beyond our objective to a copse where we could see movement when I suddenly heard a – by now familiar – CRACK. I had stupidly allowed my tank to get into the field of fire of an anti-tank gun – a 75 mm – whilst I was in the open. It appeared to be about 800 yards away but I was unable to see exactly where it was to engage it; so, realising that it would take me some time to get under cover, I told my driver to use every ounce of horsepower he had to get us back; fortunately we just managed it, but not before the tank was hit twice in the turret; as luck would have it the impact was at such a narrow angle that neither shot penetrated. They did, however, make such deep holes in the armour that the tank was eventually evacuated; the other tank with me was unscathed. Not for the first time was I grateful that the Cromwell tank, despite its poor armour, had such speed and manoeuvrability.

Our advance into Belgium and Holland, like that through France, was mainly peppered with small actions which, though on an insignificant scale in the context of the Army's overall operations, usually seemed big to the individual squadron undertaking them. However, since so many were similar in nature to those already described, I do not propose to recount them in detail. It is, however, perhaps worth saying something at this stage of our contacts with the French, Belgian and Dutch civilians.

The towns and villages through which we advanced were mostly inhabit-ed and, in all these countries, the local people gave us the most enormous help. They helped us over intelligence, telling us how far we were likely to get without meeting enemy – and often fairly exactly where we were likely to meet trouble. If they felt reasonably secure they would come out of their houses and give us an unbelievable welcome. If we planned to remain overnight they often – most generously, because they had little enough themselves – gave us food and drink. Of course, they were intensely relieved to be 'liberated', but such help and kindness was also very encouraging for us – and made what we were doing seem even more worth while. The attitude of these people was not merely kind, however, it was frequently very courageous. It was by no means unknown for us to advance leaving a village we had captured temporarily unoccupied, due to the speed at which things were moving; in these circumstances Germans sometimes managed to return and they were invariably vicious to the inhabitants.

We did not take part in the Nijmegen-Arnheim operation, but, since we were a reserve division and might be called upon for assistance, we took a keen interest; the Guards Armoured Division had moved to Nijmegen where the U.S. airborne forces had captured the bridge over the River Waal, and were trying to force a way north to relieve the 1st Airborne Division at Arnheim. At one stage I drove in my dingo behind the guards as they advanced and saw first hand what a hammering they had had. There were burnt-out tanks everywhere on both sides of the road; and, desperately though they seem to have tried, it had been virtually impossible for them to manoeuvre off the road itself, since much of it was flanked by canals or low-lying swampy country. This, of course, made the tanks a sitting target for German tank guns pointing straight down the road, and these, as I have explained, were greatly superior to our own both in effective range and in armour protection.

During the next few weeks the role of the Regiment within 7th Armoured Division was the clearance of the numerous 'pockets' of resistance by Germans which still existed all over Holland, preparatory to our advance across the river Rhine and into Germany.

We spent two weeks in late December 1944 and early January 1945 in and around the Dutch town of Sittard. It was incredibly cold and there was deep snow on the ground throughout the period; since we were positioned in open fields and sometimes slept alongside our tanks, it was a major problem to keep warm. Luckily for us the authorities had just produced a 'tank suit' which was being issued to all crews; it was a sort of overall, but very warm, waterproof and comfortable. We slept well in these in the snow. Despite the extreme cold it was a pleasant break and a welcome one; since leaving

Normandy we had not had a period long enough out of the action to maintain the tanks thoroughly and to get up replacements. For a long time the squadron had been below strength and this was now put right, so that we could play our full part in the next big operation.

Chapter 7

Life in a tank during the advance

In the 1st Royal Tanks we were equipped with Cromwell tanks. These had a crew of four – driver, gunner, radio operator and tank commander. Each had a short 75 mm gun, not to be confused with the German 75 mm gun in the Panther tank which was long and vastly more powerful; but our tanks were, as we have seen, very fast and manoeuvrable. A troop had three such tanks; there were five troops and a Squadron Headquarters (of four tanks). These, together with some twenty-five 'soft' administrative vehicles, comprised the armoured squadron. At a later stage a few Sherman tanks, especially fitted with seventeen-pounder anti-tank guns, were issued in view of the disparity between the power of our guns and those of the enemy. These (known as Fireflies) added to the squadron strength and they were far more effective against the German tanks than the Cromwells – but there were very few of them.

As a tank crew our lives revolved entirely around our individual tanks. In these we kept everything we needed – food, water and our 'bedding rolls' containing perhaps a blanket, groundsheet and washing materials; there might also be an odd bottle of brandy if one happened to come across such a thing. The food was in the form of a box of 'composite' rations – some of it dehydrated to take up as little space as possible, together with bully beef, rice pudding, tea, milk and sugar; the milk, of course, being powdered. The tank's equipment included a small primus stove and we made cooking utensils out of old tins. Our 'plates' were mess tins – deep square aluminium tins with handles; each officer and man was issued with one of these.

During pauses in operations, if we had some indication that we might be twenty minutes or more in the same place, the crew would get out the primus, tea and a 'brew can' (old tin) and brew up a cup of tea for themselves; it was a welcome break, particularly on cold days. As dark fell we were nearly always ordered to discontinue the advance and to find a

26

place as secure as possible – perhaps a wood, a field off the beaten track or even a small village. Directly we halted we posted guards round the squadron perimeter; all, including myself as squadron leader, would take their turn at guard duty throughout the night. Within our perimeter we made room for our 'soft' vehicles which came up each night that it was safe to do so with petrol, rations, ammunition and our mail, if any had arrived. As soon as they arrived the senior N.C.O. fitter would go round and ascertain from each tank crew any mechanical defects. These would then be worked on – often all night – and in the morning I would be given a detailed account of the condition of every tank. I could then report to Regimental Headquarters what my fighting strength would be. Whilst all the work of replenishment and tank maintenance was going on, the squadron leaders would normally be called to a meeting at R.H.Q. where the Colonel would give us orders for the following day; when we returned to our squadrons we, in our turn, gave orders to the five troop leaders. After this we bedded down by our tanks and got as much sleep as we could.

As can be seen, relations within the tank crew were very close, friendly and trusting. On one evening, after we had been fighting continuously for six or seven days and were all tired, we were about to settle down for the night – to be interrupted hopefully only by our appointed period of guard duty – when my tank gunner (Corporal Clarke) came to me and said that he wanted a word. He told me that he and the other two members of the crew (the driver and radio operator) had discussed the night's arrangements and had decided that I must not, on this occasion, do my share of guard duty. Of course I told him to go away and mind his own business. However, he persisted, and said, 'Look here, Major, if you make a ***** of tomorrow's battle we shall all suffer; if one of us is a bit more tired you will hardly notice the difference!' He was strictly speaking disgracefully insubordinate, but the crew's spirit was splendid – and the incident indicated a far deeper discipline than that tied rigidly to obedience of orders.

The advance was usually resumed at 'first light' so sleep was limited, particularly in summer. We would get up about an hour before H-Hour (the time we were ordered to re-start the advance); we would cook some breakfast or at least brew up a cup of tea. We had then to attend to the calls of nature – probably in the corner of the wood or field we were in – with the aid of a spade which we carried on our tanks. About twenty minutes before H-Hour we would mount our tanks, warm the engines, check the suspensions and tracks to make quite sure they were correctly adjusted and check the guns and ammunition. Possibly the most important part of the routine was to tune in (known as 'netting') the radio sets, since good communications were such an essential need in an armoured unit. Each of these tasks was undertaken by the appropriate member of the crew, the tank commander overseeing the precautions to ensure that nothing was omitted.

As the advance started we normally moved down roads or tracks for speed; one troop (a different one each day as it was a demanding and frequently dangerous role) would be ordered to lead the squadron. Squadron H.Q. would come next and the four other (reserve) troops behind. Nearly always, after a short time, we made some degree of contact with the enemy. Sometimes it might be a small detachment – perhaps some infantry in a personnel carrier with a few motor cycles; on other occasions it would be something more solid – possibly two or three tanks or self-propelled guns which could, with their superior guns, inflict enormous damage on our Cromwell tanks if these were caught in the open. If the enemy resistance was quite minor the leading troop would deal with it with its own fire power, then continue the advance as soon as possible. If, on the other hand, the opposition was clearly substantial the troop would 'fan' out off the road under cover, keeping the enemy under observation. At that stage I would go forward in my dingo to speak to the troop leader and to see the situation at first hand; if I did not consider he could deal quickly with the enemy position I would make a plan to outflank it by using my reserve troops (or some of them) to move across country. Often I would accompany the outflanking troops to ensure that they got to the right place to engage the enemy effectively. By this means the enemy position could often be dislodged and the advance continued. If all our efforts failed, and we started sustaining heavy losses, the Commanding Officer would almost certainly come forward and would bring in another squadron, or possibly supporting infantry or guns to assist. We were required to keep going at all costs, and enemy resistance had to be overcome without much delay or there would be sharp criticism on the radio from our Brigade H.Q. Despite any plea that one was incurring heavy losses and was therefore being a bit more cautious, the instruction from above was always the same – 'Sorry, but you must press on regardless.' The phrase 'pocket of resistance' is rather a misnomer; it was usually a small but very well-armed mixed group of tanks, guns and infantry. They were normally sited on a main approach road, or in a wood or village which it was difficult for us to circumvent. Because we often ran into them without much warning we had casualties quite out of proportion to the size and importance of many of these actions. Perhaps it is understandable therefore that, as we approached towns or villages, we often used incendiary machine gun ammunition and set fire to the houses in the path of our intended advance. This, of course, did cause much damage and hardship to the Dutch or Belgian people who lived there, and it seemed a poor reward for all their kindness to us; unfortunately it was frequently the only way of avoiding heavier casualties, or even having our advance checked altogether.

There were two such minor operations, amongst what became almost a daily routine at the time, which may be worth mentioning as examples. My squadron was ordered to advance up a road and capture the small town of Dinther (near S'Hertogenbosch in Holland) which was known to contain a strong detachment of enemy tanks. The advance itself went without much incident except for a certain amount of mortaring (but this did not bother us as long as we stayed in our tanks) and some sniping. Many tank commanders were killed by snipers as they invariably had their heads outside the turret when on the move to get a better view, but this time we were lucky. After about two hours, and with the help of an infantry company which had been placed under my command, we cleared the town and all seemed quiet. As a precaution against an enemy counter attack from S'Hertogenbosch I quickly stationed my tank troops round the edge of the town. I did this by radio; I then set off on foot to see each troop on the ground and to ensure that all possible enemy approaches had been covered. In the case of one particular troop I had to cross a field diagonally – a walk of about 400 to 500 yards – in the open. When I was halfway across I was conscious of some movement in rough grass on my left and, through the corner of my eye, saw six men – Germans – lying in a line about thirty yards away with their rifles trained on me! I suppose I should not have been too perturbed, as any attempt to shoot me would have brought the troop I was visiting into action and short shrift for the Germans; but I did not think this would help me! So I walked the remaining 200 yards with as slow and steady pace as I could muster, trying to pretend that I had not got a care in the world, until I was within shouting distance of the nearest tank (which had not so far noticed what was going on). The Germans were then rounded up and taken prisoner.

The other incident occurred in late January near the small town of Echt, near Maesek on the river Meuse. We were told to occupy the town, together with the neighbouring village of Schilburg, and to clear them of enemy. The advance to Echt presented no difficulty which was just as well as we were, as so often in Holland, flanked on each side by a large ditch (canal is probably a more apt description). In the middle of Schilburg, however, the leading troop came under heavy anti-tank gun fire, and the first two tanks went up in flames in a matter of twenty seconds. In an attempt to ascertain exactly where the enemy gun was, I got out of my tank and went up to the top floor of a house, taking with me an extension (remote control) lead to my tank radio set below; from this position I could clearly see what appeared to be a Panther tank (one of the Germans' most modern and powerful) some 800 yards straight down the road ahead of us. I summoned up the second troop to engage it and, as soon as they opened fire, I could detect direct hits on the armour of the Panther by the red glows at the point where the shots made contact with, but did not penetrate, the armour. The Panther continued firing and, in a few minutes, the second troop had lost two of its tanks – one by a direct hit and the other bogged down in a deep ditch trying to outflank the enemy. I tried with a third troop, endeavouring to get at the Panther from a slightly different angle so as to attack its side (and thinner) armour; but I continued to lose tanks at an alarming rate and, by nightfall, seven were out of action – either destroyed or hopelessly bogged. Just before dark and for no obvious reason, the Panther withdrew; so we seemed to have frightened him if nothing else, but at considerable cost. Fortunately most of our crews were saved.

We again learned a lesson that day that our Cromwell tanks, despite their considerable speed and manoeuvrability, were no match for a single German tank with a modern 75 mm gun (which the Panther had), provided it was well sited so that its flanks were protected and with a good field of fire straight down a road.

We stayed where we were for the night. The following morning I heard some firing from the far end of the village and went forward about 500 yards on foot to see where it was coming from. Crawling along a hedge I managed to get a fair idea as to where the enemy were, and I turned to return to the Squadron. As I did so I was subjected to a burst of machine gun fire; the enemy had obviously located me and I had to crawl the whole way back on my tummy to avoid presenting them with a target. As it was it became a very uncomfortable move as the periodic bursts of fire seemed to be just above me and I was certain that any error on my part would be disastrous. However, I was lucky and got back safely; the only casualty was my web belt containing my revolver, which I lost during the crawl.

During all these operations we did, of course, take a considerable number of prisoners; since we had no means of looking after or controlling them we simply instructed them to walk back up the road towards our Divisional Headquarters, where there were facilities for handling them. Their morale was usually pretty low by this time and they all seemed to do as they were told; it would certainly have been quite easy for a prisoner to escape if he had really wanted to do so.

1936 – HOVE. Diana, Cynthia, Pamela, Jock, Iain and my Mother.

Pam, Self, Jock and Iain. Le Zoute 1938. Belgium.

1939, near Libyan border. Officers' sleeping quarters.

1939. The desert flooded after heavy rain.

Our Wedding in Newbury March 1940.

Phyll Lloyd (my aunt), myself, my mother, John (my brother).

Parents at our wedding – my Mother, Philip Henstock, 'Winks' Henstock, my Father.

Investiture at Buckingham Palace in 1944. Left to right: Sergeant T. Harland, DCM., Sergeant H. Bennett, MM., Sergeant J. Wacouuachie, MM., Sergeant F. Williams, MM and WO2 Macgregor, MM., all of the Royal Tank Regiment. Credit Caption: 'Tank Magazine'.

'A' Squadron 1st Royal Tank Regiment 1944.

WO2 Bob Macgregor being presented with the DCM in 1945.
Credit Caption: Imperial War Museum.

Dome Church – British Mk V tank captured in WW 1 in foreground.

Emperor's Palace

Chancellery – The position where Hitler and Eva Braun were found.

Montgomery of Alamein
Field-Marshal

'A' Mess HQ 30 Corps 1945 Monty comes to lunch. General Sir Brian Horrocks with Field Marshal Montgomery and the officers of the Mess.

Detmold 1946 – Main Gate Guard turned out for the General's visit.

Marriage of Richard and Elizabeth Ward. I was the best man. 1947.

Chapter 8

Leave in England

Leave (forty-eight hours in the U.K.) was started in January 1945 and, since my squadron was in need of so many replacement tanks, I was one of the first to go. Before I went home I had the sad experience of seeing the Commanding Officer of the 5th Royal Tanks, Gus Holliman, one of the most courageous and nicest men I have ever met, killed. He had come up to Schilburg in a dingo to reconnoitre the situation as the 5th R. Tanks were due to take over the advance from the 1st. He had just driven past the point where I had engaged the Panther the day before and, suddenly, there was a shot from his front and he and his dingo were destroyed. It may have been the same Panther which had inflicted so much damage on my Squadron, firing one shot and then withdrawing; we never knew for certain.

In those days, since there was no other way of spending one's pay, I found that I could afford to go to the Savoy Hotel in London when on leave, so I met Pam there for our forty-eight hours. My father was at his flat at 97 Cadogan Gardens, so I telephoned him to say where we were; he said he had a small party on that evening: 'Why not come and join it?' So we did. When we arrived we found Mr. Gwilym Lloyd George, the Minister of Fuel and Power and later Home Secretary; Mr. Duncan Sandys, the Minister of Works, and Mr. Rab Sinclair, the Chief Executive at the Ministry of Production (and also the President of the Imperial Tobacco Company); their wives and many others who were in or who were close to the government at that time. Rab Sinclair had been told by my father why I had obtained leave at this juncture – and how inferior our tanks were both in armour and armament to those of the Germans. He crossed the room to where I was standing – with some menace in his eyes – and sharply accused me of having an unjustified lack of faith in our tanks, and of a lack of tactical skill; 'You should go round and attack them in the flank,' he said. I pointed to the canals which frequently ran on both sides of the roads in

31

Holland, and explained that I had actually seen our shells, fired at short range, bouncing off a German tank which had been able to destroy so much of my squadron with virtual impunity. He was, however, quite uninterested in explanations; only anxious to shut me up. Hearing this conversation Gwilym Lloyd George, a delightful man, came up to me and said, 'Take no notice of him; I myself have had an experience of armchair politicians like him during the 1914 war when I myself was at the front. They have no idea whatever of what actually goes on and make a lot of fatuous pronouncements from their cosy Whitehall offices.' He suggested that I ask Rab Sinclair to come out to Holland and spend a few days with the squadron. So, when I again saw Rab Sinclair to say goodbye, I did just that; I received no proper reply – simply rather a cold 'good-bye'.

The following day I received a telephone call from Mr. (later Sir Claude) Gibb, the Chairman of the Tank Board, asking if I would call at his office. I felt I should do so despite the fact that I was losing precious hours of my leave. I located the building, just off the Strand, and walked into an enormous office. A pleasant man, who turned out to be Mr. Gibb, came forward to meet me; he was accompanied by a Major General Charles Dunphie, a gunner who was senior armoured adviser at the Ministry of Supply. Mr. Gibb explained very quietly that he had been told that I had made statements criticising the quality of our tanks; he had, he said, asked me to come and see him so that he could explain and assure me that they were every bit as good as the best German tanks. He then took me to examine a number of charts and graphs which hung on his wall which, he maintained, proved his point conclusively – that the 75 mm shells from our Cromwell tanks DID penetrate the front armour of the largest German tanks. I told him that no chart could explain how, if that was true, I could have lost so many tanks – all through penetration of the Cromwell's front armour – whilst securing repeated hits on the German Panther which did not penetrate. So, mutually unconvinced, we parted and I returned to Holland the following day. On my way back I could not help reflecting that my forty-eight hour leave might not have done my career much good but that, if I got the sack for speaking 'out of turn', I would be saved a good deal of inconvenience – not to mention the odd fright!

Chapter 9

Germany

We were not directly involved in the operation to cross the river Rhine. After the airborne assault it became largely an infantry operation; clearing German units from the approaches to the pontoon bridges which had been constructed, and holding the bridgehead itself so that the bulk of the Army could cross. In the 1st Royal Tanks we crossed at Wesel, and then (with the rest of 7th Armoured Division) moved quickly to concentrate in the area Borken – Stadtlohn, just across the river.

For some hours all was quiet – suspiciously so! However, after what seemed an age, I received a radio message to continue the advance up the road which led north-east towards the town of Rheine. I soon began to see the reason for the apparent hesitation on the part of our Divisional H.Q. We advanced in our usual formation, one troop leading, then Squadron H.Q. and then the remaining four troops. After we had been moving for a few minutes the road took us through a thick and extensive wood; and, as we entered it, the whole immediate area became like an inferno. Anti-tank guns were firing at us down the road, and bazookas from within the wood at our flanks; there appeared to be Germans everywhere and we had obviously stumbled on a substantial enemy position. Three of my tanks were hit, two catching fire; within minutes none of us could see anything in the dense smoke. So I was ordered to withdraw the Squadron to a point just outside the wood with a view to finding another way round.

Such was the scene when a call on my radio summoned me to meet my C.O. (Pat Hobart) about half a mile away; I got into my dingo with my maps, etc., and drove to the rendezvous where I met the other squadron leaders, the Royal Artillery support regimental commander and the C.O. of the 1/5 Queens, the infantry battalion which had been detailed to work with us. The C.O. explained the seriousness and the urgency of the position. The Ruhr, to our south, was proving a very tough nut; the advance of the Allied formations fighting in this area had been slowed almost to a halt. To the north of us the ground was cut up with canals and, as a result, the Germans were finding it relatively easy to slow down the division advancing on this front. Yet speed was clearly absolutely essential and, extraordinary though it seemed to us at the time, our present line of advance appeared to Army H.Q. to be the only practicable one if we were to get forward quickly. He went on to say that, since we had not been able to advance through the wood in front of us by day, we had been instructed to try and do so by night. I was to make a further attempt to get down the road I was already on; and B Squadron would move on a parallel road on my right. Realising the difficult task that he had set us, he allotted both squadrons a company of infantry and a Royal Artillery forward observation officer who could call on the fire of a twenty-five pounder regiment or indeed the whole Divisional Artillery. He made it clear to both of us that, if we were completely stopped, we could use these supporting units to help to protect ourselves until daylight. Concluding, he said that we could each choose our starting time but that we should inform him in due course what we had decided.

By the end of the conference it was about 7.00 p.m. and, as I drove back to my squadron, three problems persisted in my mind. Firstly, how to get back into the wood when there were two of my tanks (still burning) practically blocking its entrance; secondly, having got in, how to brush aside the enemy guns and bazookas at night having failed to do so in daylight; and, thirdly, how best to explain to the squadron the awkward task we had been set. All these difficulties seemed to be compounded by the fact that our training in the past had been that tanks simply do not fight at night – it was always considered that they were too vulnerable. However, our orders were clear and we were going to attack that night whether we liked it or not; our objective was to be the small town of Ahaus, about seven miles on down the road.

I met my troop leaders, the gunner officer and the infantry company commander; I had already decided that the latter two should travel in my own tank and, for this to be possible, I temporarily ejected my tank gunner and my radio operator. I then put it to my troop leaders and to the two supporting arms that it seemed to me that there was only one really good plan to adopt; we would have to go fast – very fast. We had, through a careful foot reconnaissance, ascertained that a way could just be found between the two burning tanks. The tanks of my squadron would lead the advance, moving one by one through this gap, followed by the infantry who were mounted in kangaroos (armoured tracked personnel carriers). From the moment the first tank went through the gap we aimed to keep the enemy from firing at us effectively by concentrating intense machine gun fire from every tank (except my own as I had no gunner) on the ground about twenty yards from the road on both sides; we decided to use a high proportion of incendiary ammunition which could burn most houses the enemy might be occupying as strong points; this would also serve to light up the road in front of us. We were not going to use lights on the tanks, but would rely on the fires lit by the incendiary ammunition and the small amount of moonlight we expected that night. We thought that to use the tanks' headlights would give an enemy gun sited to fire straight down the road a good aiming mark; but, to neutralise any such gun, the leading tank was – in addition – to fire an occasional round of armour-piercing ammunition straight ahead 'on spec' from time to time. We thought we could be ready by 1.00 a.m. and made this our 'H Hour'; I informed my C.O. accordingly on the radio.

Such was the plan; a pretty hit-or-miss affair but, by the time we were due to start, we were all fully confident that it would work. To aid this confidence we gave each man a tot of brandy from a stock I had been collecting.

At 1.00 a.m. we started off as arranged. Within minutes the area to our front was like a firework display; the quantity of ammunition being poured into the narrow strip of ground each side of the road was colossal, with thirteen tanks (my strength was down to fourteen) firing non-stop. The incendiary rounds soon started fires all over the place. Despite all this fire the enemy let off countless bazookas at us as the tanks went by, but we had clearly put them off their aim as nearly all of them missed – or at least failed to hit a vital part of a tank. What became worrying for me was that, before we had been going for very long, we started to lose an increasing number of tanks which, unable to see their way clearly, left the road and got stuck; so, as soon as I realised what was happening, I ordered all tanks to use headlights. This made the 'display' even more striking and I learned afterwards that it attracted an impressive audience, including the Divisional Commander who watched from a hill near Stadtlohn.

By 5.00 a.m. I was, myself, in Ahaus with one other tank of my Squadron H.Q. and two other tanks – four tanks altogether; we had, however, broken through the German position completely and I felt that we would be able to hold the town for a short time. I reported accordingly to my C.O. During the next hour or so many of the other tanks came down the road one by one. Several had become ditched but had managed to get back on the road. By 8.00 a.m., I was able to report that I had eleven tanks disposed around the perimeter of Ahaus. In the three tanks we had lost the previous day we had had two men killed and three wounded – fortunately not seriously, amazingly, during the night attack itself we had no personnel casualties whatever. However, many tanks had been hit and would need repair; my own was hit on the mudguard, but I felt that I could well do without that!

In the meantime, unfortunately, on the right hand road, B Squadron had run into a lot of trouble and had sustained heavy casualties – including the Squadron second-in-command and another officer, both of whom were killed. The reserve – C Squadron – had been sent down this road to help them, but had also failed to make progress. Thus we, in A Squadron, were well out into enemy territory unsupported – and we felt we had earned a rest! Our feelings, however, were not shared by the Divisional Commander who ordered the Regiment to continue the advance immediately, and to capture the village of Heek – a further seven miles on. Since B Squadron clearly could not do this, and as C Squadron were by now hopelessly bogged down on the parallel road trying to help them get out without further casualties, the job of getting to Heek fell to my squadron.

We had had a report from the 11th Hussars, who always did a superb job as the divisional armoured car regiment and who were consistently reliable in their reconnaissance reports, that there was a heavy German gun just ahead; they reported it as being about 1,000 yards from our position in Ahaus, well concealed and sited to fire up the road at us as soon as we started moving forwards. They added that they believed it was not alone and that there could be several – tanks or self-propelled guns – in the position. We were, of course, fairly tired by now and bright thoughts as to how to deal with such problems came but slowly. However, I had, as one of my troop leaders, a splendid, recently commissioned warrant officer – Lt. Bob Mcgregor – whose troop had been in reserve and had not taken an active part in the previous night's operation; so I called him up and asked him to try and make his way to a farm building on a rise to our left front, from which point I hoped he might be able to engage the enemy gun from the flank. Alternatively I wondered if a way could be found to get forward across country and out of sight of the enemy gun. Whilst he was moving forward I arranged for the other tanks of the Squadron to make sufficient noise on the road to make it appear as if we were advancing by the direct route. As soon as Bob had got to the farm building I led the rest of the squadron and the infantry company up to join him; he pointed out the place where he thought the gun was – perhaps still – situated but said that he thought he could find a way forward well out of its sight. I followed immediately behind him, leaving the remaining troops and the infantry at the farm. After going about 1,000 yards we found a good deal of cover and it was clear to me that we could probably get down from the rise we were on to the main road not far from Heek itself. So I called up the rest of the squadron and the company of 1/6 Queens and led them accordingly; when we got into Heek we captured a number of German soldiers and made them prisoners; one of them told us that one Tiger tank and three self-propelled guns had withdrawn and were moving to Rheine. The main brunt of this successful operation was borne by Bob Macgregor's troop; not only did he lead for much of the way but he exercised incredible skill in finding a covered approach between enemy detachments. His ability and coolness saved the squadron many casualties and for this I recommended him for a Military Cross (to add to his Distinguished Conduct and Military Medals). He was killed tragically a week later; a gun in another tank of his troop was loaded when it should not have been and it was accidentally discharged into the back of Bob's tank. He was the best troop leader I have ever had the good fortune to serve with; and he had been through the whole desert campaign as well as that of North-West Europe.

Three other first class troop leaders who had also served in the 'ranks' were Captains (Conky) Harland, Tommy Stanton and Paddy McKee; all these promoted warrant officers, and doubtless many others in different regiments, proved outstanding in the battle. One other troop leader in my squadron who had served with particular distinction throughout these battles – and who continued to do so till the end of the war – was Captain (later Brigadier) H.B.C. (Brian) Watkins; his father had been in the Regiment before him. It was noticeable that, when the fighting was at its most intense, Brian was never far away; he was of great help and support to me.

We had, of course, arrived in Heek entirely across country, without using the road at all. After we had been there some minutes the C.O. spoke to me on the radio and asked me to send a troop back down the road to Ahaus to ensure that it was quite clear of enemy guns or mines, so that other units could be sent forward by this route. Later he came up himself to Heek; he told me that all other efforts to advance along the divisional front were proving slow, if not impossible, and that the greater part of 12th Corps (at this time our parent formation) would be coming through the gap we had managed to create, within the next few hours.

Shortly the squadron was comfortably established in various houses in Heek; and, later that evening, we were able to see an apparently endless stream of tanks, lorries and cars thundering past the small village houses. By a stroke of good fortune the house I had made into my squadron headquarters had hot water laid on, and I was able to have a bath – the first for many days and very welcome.

Several days later, we in the 1st found ourselves again in the forefront of the advance; as we approached the river Weser my squadron was directed on to the town of Hoya, just south of Verden. My C.O. told me that the river bridge here was believed to be still intact, and that I was to rush it and establish a bridgehead beyond it. As my first troop entered the town, however, there was an enormous explosion, and the air was full of the resultant debris; the Germans had withdrawn, and as they did so, had demolished the bridge. It was, without doubt, a failure on our part but I must confess to a feeling of some relief as the bridge went up; it is a nasty experience to cross a largish river, knowing that you might well be cut off from any support. Eventually we were withdrawn from Hoya and we crossed the River Weser on a pontoon bridge at Verden which had already been captured. The following day we were again sent forward to lead the Division, and we pursued the enemy to Dorfmark, Soltau and then northwards towards Hamburg.

Our daily routine during this advance through Germany was much as I have described earlier, but one incident was amusing (though it might have been anything but amusing). We nearly always started to move forward at first light – and then to go as fast and as far as possible during the day; in the evening we would stop for replenishment. Here we were punctilious about placing adequate guards out – even more so than we had been in France, Belgium and Holland where there were friendly populations; in Germany there were elements of enemy units scattered everywhere and one never quite knew when one was safe. On one such evening we had re-fuelled the tanks, taken on ammunition and fed ourselves; most of us had gone to bed when the duty radio operater came to me and said that the C.O. wanted to speak to me urgently. He told me that the Regimental Headquarters of the 5th Royal Inniskilling Dragoon Guards (known as the 'Skins') who were in the same brigade, and who had stopped for the night about five miles from us, were being attacked; and I was to send a troop of tanks down the road to help see off the intruders. This I did; later I learned what had happened. Like us, the Skins had re-fuelled, and had then settled down to sleep; they were in a small village and the R.H.Q. was comfortably placed in a house. Satisfied with their day the C.O., Second-in-Command and Adjutant had opened a bottle of Champagne; unfortunately, however, they had omitted to place sufficient guards around the village and, whilst they were consuming their bottle – and quite disturbingly suddenly – the brickwork of one of the walls of the house cracked and started to crumble.

Through the hole came slowly the barrel of a large gun. It looked like a German 75 mm gun; indeed, that is just what it was! A German tank seemed to have got lost, but how and why he drove straight into the wall of the house was never known – at least not to us. The Champagne party was, as can be imagined, sharply broken up and luckily the worst of the possible consequences were avoided as the enemy tank disappeared into the night as soon as he heard the noise of my troop appearing. Apart from being a regiment of our brigade, I was relieved that all was well as the Second-in-Command was a very good friend of mine and I would not have liked anything untoward to have happened to him.

We took part in one other operation before the war ended. Just south of Hamburg and, again, in a very wooded area we ran into a strong German unit; as so often they were armed with some guns and a considerable number of bazookas. My leading tank was hit, effectively blocking the road; I managed to get the surviving members of its crew out and onto the back of the tanks of the reserve troop, but I felt I had to get my squadron out of the wood and try to find a better way forward – possibly across country. Whilst turning round in order to withdraw, we came under increased fire and, sadly, my Second-in-Command's tank – which was a few yards behind my own – was hit by a bazooka and he was killed. I felt this particularly badly as he was an officer of the 3rd Carabiniers, George Cordy Simpson; he had been attached to our Regiment for about six months.

An hour later we were able to re-enter this bazooka-ridden wood and cleared a passage through it so that we could move on to Hamburg. I had a message from Pat Hobart to meet him on the autobahn (the first I had ever seen) just south of Hamburg. During our conversation we were suddenly heavily shelled by German 88 mm guns which had spotted us. The shells were landing on the carriageway and exploding all over the place; so we moved smartly into a ditch nearby to talk. It was the last time I was shelled during the war which ended ten days later. It was at this rather dramatic moment that he told me that I was to receive an immediate award of the Military Cross.

Just as the war ended, in May 1945, I was posted as Second-in-Command of the 141st Regiment, Royal Armoured Corps; this was a Crocodile (Churchill tanks armed with flame throwers) Regiment. I stayed there about four months, after which they were disbanded.

This Regiment were stationed on a disused airfield at Rotenburg, between Bremen and Hamburg. One of the most interesting incidents to occur during my short stay with the Regiment was that the Guards Armoured Division chose this as the site for their final parade, before they themselves were disbanded. The Parade was entitled 'Farewell to Armour' and it was most impressive and moving. All the tank units were lined up, moved in dead straight lines past the saluting base and drove slowly (still in their long straight lines) away and over the slope of the airfield till they were out of sight; whilst they were moving away the band played 'Auld Lang Syne'. The crews then quickly dismounted from their tanks and, after a short period, the same men reappeared over the horizon – marching; they passed the saluting base and took up positions where the tanks had originally been. This was all done in quick time with a precision one could only expect to see on the Horse Guards Parade; But, when one considers that the airfield grass was rough with numerous tufts, potholes and other impediments, all of us who watched came to the conclusion that we had never seen anything of the sort done so well and so imaginatively. The Guards Armoured Division may not have been the most brilliant of our formations but they were certainly very brave, as they had showed at Nijmegen; in ceremonial, no one who was at Rotenburg that day would doubt that they are quite unsurpassed.

Chapter 10

Peace – and life in postwar Germany

The war was now over, at least in Europe. We had been prepared to hear that there would be widespread posting of officers and men to the Far East, to take part in the war against Japan; but the atom bombs dropped on Hiroshima and Nagasaki altered all this. Instead, Allied military units all over Europe concentrated on disbandment or – in the case of regular units – reorganising for a peacetime role. I was intensely sad to leave the 1st Tanks where I had so many friends; but I must honestly admit that it was a relief to be out of the constant shelling and the feeling that one could not relax for an instant if one was not to be a target for an enemy anti-tank gun. Above all, there was the strain of being the leading tank moving down a road into enemy territory; and the constant thought that, as your tank turned a corner, there might be a loud 'CRACK' – the noise of a powerful anti-tank gun discharging a shell in your direction. Any such feelings of apprehension were, however, balanced by the fact that a battle keeps one incredibly busy; and, being a 'team' – and all in it together – certainly provides a sort of exhilaration, which is difficult for those who have not had the experience to understand.

In September 1945, after my spell with 141 Regiment R.A.C., I was posted to H.Q. 30 Corps temporarily. Here, amongst other duties, I had to prepare for families to come out and join us in Germany. This was a necessary move from every point of view, but it was made even more important due to the strict non-fraternisation rule which General Montgomery had imposed – to bring home to the Germans the disgrace in which they were held. This necessary rule did, however, make life very dull for the troops who, in the early days were not allowed to enter shops, cinemas, hotels or any German Institution and who were, therefore, virtually confined to their camps.

Families eventually started arriving in the autumn of 1946, and the

41

organisation needed to provide for them was considerable. To begin with there was a substantial movement problem; Cuxhaven was used as the port of entry almost exclusively during the first three to four months, when the number of wives and children arriving was extremely large. Transit camps suitable for women and children were set up at Cuxhaven; they were also set up at various other points in the British Zone of Germany for those who might not be able to get to their unit on the day they disembarked, or for whom there was no immediately available accommodation. Schools were, of course, needed within reach of all the main barracks and in addition two boarding schools were established. The sudden increase in the size of the population of the British Zone, resulting from the arrival of so many families, necessitated the extension of hospitals; it also involved a sharp increase in the workload of every unit medical officer in the Zone. NAAFI canteens had already been set up in all barracks, but more were now needed; and shops, stocked to meet every foreseeable requirement, were provided at convenient points. There were also 'clubs' (NAAFI-run restaurants) set up all over the Zone – both for officers and for N.C.O.s. The NAAFI has not always had a good reputation in these matters but there is no doubt that some of these clubs were excellent – the '21 Club' at Bad Oeynhausen and the Club at Bad Salzuflen, near Bielefeld, becoming particularly well known for their high standard.

All this did, of course, create a need for a vast increase in the availability of transport. Hitherto regiments had only a small number of jeeps and there was little else except ordinary load-carrying trucks of one kind or another. These were, however, very basic and they had no seats, so many had to be modified to make them more comfortable. Such vehicles were then allocated for the use of wives and children to take them to hospital, to the NAAFI shop or perhaps to visit another unit.

Since no fraternisation with the German population was allowed, all entertainment had to be provided within the barracks itself, and families (who mainly lived outside barracks) had to make many journeys from their homes to the barracks for the limited sport and entertainment which could be arranged. Houses were requisitioned from the Germans; some were furnished, usually sparsely. In the case of those without any furniture this had to be provided; H.Q. British Army of the Rhine had therefore commandeered a furniture factory to turn out suitable beds, tables, chairs and other basic items. These were then issued to units throughout the Zone as needed.

For both officers and men – and indeed their families – there were outstanding sporting facilities. The barracks were mostly well equipped in this (and every other) respect and, for those who were interested, there was excellent pheasant, partridge and duck shooting available – all at very low cost; there was also superb trout fishing; I myself learned to fish there and I have always been grateful for the opportunity. There were a number of residential leave centres at Ehrwald in Austria, Bad Harzburg and Winterburg, the latter two being in Germany; these provided skiing, and there were good arrangements for the instruction of beginners. There were also a number of sailing clubs at various lakes. All these facilities were open to all ranks and families were particularly encouraged to make use of them.

As no member of the occupying forces was allowed to have any dealing with the German shops, or to trade in any way with them, local currency (the Reichsmark) was of no use to us; indeed, the currency was so inflated that it was of precious little use to the Germans either. However, fairness dictates that I must confess that there was, despite all the rules, a thriving black market; cigarettes were the main 'currency' and they were used to purchase – illegally – those things the Germans could provide such as vegetables and other produce. Later, in order to give the Forces a currency they could legally and usefully spend, British Armed Forces Vouchers (B.A.F.V.s) were printed in various denominations and were legal tender for NAAFI and Leave Centre purchases. All this continued until about 1949 when the whole German currency was reformed and the Deutschmark introduced; by this time the non–fraternisation rule was gradually being relaxed, and civilian shops and other facilities increasingly used.

Despite the obvious frustrations of life in Germany just after the war, families were well looked after and, on the whole, very happy – possibly all the more so for having to make so much of their own recreation.

By January 1946 I had returned to the 1st Royal Tanks, this time as Second-in-Command. The Regiment was then in Berlin – in Kladow Barracks, just on the border with the Russian Zone. We spent a further four months in Berlin and, whilst there was little military training to be done there as there were constant guard duties, it was an interesting period. We set up technical training schools within the barracks to ensure that our mechanical, gunnery and radio standards were maintained. At the same time we emphasised the need for the highest possible standards of smartness and discipline, in and out of barracks. At that time we were able to drive into East Berlin and could visit without impediment the ruins of the old Reichstag building and the bunker where Hitler and Eva Braun committed suicide – and much else. There was also an increasing social life within the Allied community in the City.

In the Spring of 1946 my Regiment was offered what was probably the best barracks in the British Zone of Germany – at Detmold, near Hanover. It had been specially built by Hermann Goering for the Luftwaffe, and was currently occupied by the R.A.F. as part of their headquarters in Germany; it had, however, been decided to move them out so as to concentrate the whole R.A.F. Headquarters at Gutersloh. It was splendidly laid out, the well-equipped barrack blocks and messes being surrounded by lawns and shrubs. It was centrally heated by one enormous boiler which kept very warm every building in the camp area – including married quarters. There were lavish playing fields, tennis courts and a running track; there was also a modern cinema. The old aircraft hangars made excellent tank hangars, and there were well-designed workshops attached. Of course, the place required an enormous number of people to run it, but this presented no difficulty as we were, at that time, able to employ an almost unlimited number of Germans for any purpose we considered right. I should add that this comfortable state of affairs did not last long and, by the middle of 1947, we were under considerable pressure to reduce drastically the German staff we were employing; our government had agreed to start paying the Germans who worked for us and, unsurprisingly, the 'carte blanche' we had rapidly came to an end.

After writing to get his consent we named the barracks Hobart Barracks, after General Hobart (Pat's uncle) who had probably done more than any other single person to prepare our armoured forces for war, and to ensure that they were trained for the Normandy landing.

The day we arrived in these new barracks I learned from my Commanding Officer – John Sleeman – that the authorities had been good enough to appoint me an officer of the Order of St. John of Jerusalem.

We had been in Detmold for a little over a year when the Russians, who had always resented our presence in Berlin and (as they felt) in the middle of their Zone, closed the autobahn from Helmstedt to Berlin. This was the only authorised land access to the City open to the Allied armies. In order therefore both to maintain our garrison and also the civil population an airlift was mounted. In the case of the British Zone this was based on Gutersloh airfield near Bielefeld and Gatow airfield in the British sector of Berlin. The whole process of marshalling and loading of stores, and the reception of the many people who needed to travel to or from Berlin, involved considerable organisation; we, in the 1st Royal Tanks, were asked to assist in this and we sent to Gutersloh a squadron leader – Major Bowling Smith – together with a large detachment of soldiers for the purpose. Their assistance seems to have been appreciated, judging by the letters we received, and certainly they themselves gained a lot of experience from this highly unusual, if arduous duty. The airlift achieved its object and, though the City clearly suffered some shortages, life was maintained – as was our political position – and the Russians suddenly dropped the blockade many months later; they never tried it again.

The other two fighting squadron leaders in the Regiment at that time were Major (later General Sir Richard) Ward, G.B.E., K.C.B., D.S.O., M.C., and Major (later Lt. Colonel) Clifton Rayment, M.B.E.; Major (later Colonel) Tom Craig, M.B.E., M.C., who had been with us since the breakout from Normandy, had just left the Regiment to go to another appointment. Together these officers made a formidable team and the Regiment – as I learned when I myself left to go to Headquarters British Army of the Rhine – was considered highly efficient in every respect. We also had some excellent subalterns; mostly these were national service officers, but many took regular commissions. One of the best was Captain Joe Odam; sadly he had to leave the Army early when his father died and he was left a large farm and estate in Peterborough. He has, however, well fulfilled his promise and is now prominent in farming and in civic circles in the area; for many years he ran the East of England Agricultural Show, he was chairman of the Peterborough bench of Magistrates and did a turn as High Sherriff. He was, however, a great loss to the army.

The 7th Armoured Division, of which the Regiment were a part, was reformed for administrative purposes and re-named 'Hanover District'. It was commanded by Major General G.P.B. Roberts, C.B., D.S.O., M.C., who had a quite outstanding record as an Armoured commander both in North Africa and in North-West Europe. He was also a very popular commander and the District, consequently, was a happy one. I had known General Pip since joining the Army. He retired whilst still relatively young to take up a post in industry.

In 1948 I was appointed military assistant to the Chief of Staff at H.Q. British Army of the Rhine at Bad Oeynhausen. This was a most interesting post; the Commander in Chief (General Sir Charles Keightley) and the Chief of Staff (General Sir William Stratton) had adjoining offices and, though I had no responsibility for the social life of either (they each had their own A.D.C.s), I was in charge of the office. Unfortunately, this period was, for Pam and myself, marred by the loss of our newly born son, David – just as I was taking over the new job. Pam had had a bad time during the pregnancy and had contracted toxaemia; so the outcome was not totally unexpected. It was, however, a very sad moment for both of us.

It was a busy time in the headquarters; not only did we have to produce a plan for the defence of Germany in conditions of the utmost secrecy (less than a dozen officers were allowed to know about it at the early stage), but the plan – and the resultant deployment – had in due course to be carefully worked in with our allies. In 1949 NATO was formed and much of this planning work was taken over from us. There was, however, still a considerable amount of liaison and co-ordination needed between the Allied armies – and indeed between the three services. This, of course, led to numerous visits by staff officers – high ranking and also those at a lower level – to our headquarters at Bad Oeynhausen.

All this placed a great strain on the Commander in Chief – and indeed on the whole staff – since it was superimposed on the normal work of training and administering the army, with no additional staff. General Charles Keightley, a most capable and charming man, was perfectly cast for this awkward role; he proved well able to deal with even the most difficult of representatives of our Allies. One such visitor – indeed a very frequent visitor – was the French General, de Lattre de Tassigny. He had attained distinction both with General De Gaulle's Free French Army during the war, and also with the French Army in Indo-China; he was however extremely touchy and difficult over almost every problem that arose, and he took offence at the slightest provocation.

There were many others, too, who needed careful handling and General Charles did this with great calm and tact. I have said that I had no responsibility for the Commander in Chief's social life; he was, however, very kind to us and continually asked Pam and myself to Kostedt – his large house near the headquarters. As a host to a difficult guest he was truly a master; once, when speaking to me over a drink about some of his problems, he told me that he always placed his guests in small groups before and after dinner (and never in a large circle which he regarded as fatal). His wife, Joan, who was also a splendid hostess, would ensure that the guests were moved round from time to time, so that they did not get too settled. He usually had fifteen to twenty people to dinner, and he gave an immense amount of thought beforehand as to the best way of entertaining each individual – and of keeping them all interested. His parties smoothed many a difficult day in the office. Looking back on this period I think I learned more about entertaining from Charles Keightley than from anyone else I have ever met.

Chapter 11

'Monty'

Another frequent visitor to HQ B.A.O.R. was General (later Field Marshal) Montgomery who, when the war ended, went to the War Office as Chief of the Imperial General Staff. He had been the Commander of 21 Army group, comprising the 1st (Canadian) and 2nd (British) Armies, and indeed – for the Normandy landing itself – he was the commander of the whole Allied force under General Eisenhower. I cannot say that I knew him well personally, but I did meet him on many occasions. During my time at HQ B.A.O.R. I got to know him better than I had previously as he used my office during his visits to dictate letters and to do his telephoning. My contacts with him went back some years as he commanded the Warwickshire Regiment in Alexandria when my father commanded the Canal Brigade at Ismailia during the early 1930s; the Warwickshire Regiment was part of this Brigade.

He was, even at this time, a solider marked out for advancement, but he did some rather stupid things and was sometimes disloyal. My father believed in night training and, soon after he arrived in Egypt, he arranged a big night exercise involving the whole Brigade. Monty thought this a waste of time and he also probably considered that my father, not being an infantryman, should have consulted him first. Since the exercise was a *fait accompli*, however, Monty had to take part; however, he was determined that it should be as short as possible, and he contrived with another C.O. – Colonel Franklyn of the West Yorkshire Regiment – to bring it to an end long before my father had intended. They clearly thought that they could 'get away with it', but they soon learned their mistake as my father promptly laid on another – and bigger – night exercise a fortnight later; this time he declared in advance the time it would end.

Even at this relatively young age Monty was confident that every problem must have a clear-cut military solution. My father told me that, in

47

Alexandria, when faced with the number of soldiers who contracted V.D., he decided to start a military brothel; and, in order to ensure that this was free of disease, he ordered his Medical Officer to inspect the girls. In the event the M.O. refused to do this as he did not consider it part of his duty; so Monty threatened him with a Court Martial. There was, of course, no ordinary fuss. Members of Parliament, the press and all kinds of other bodies got to hear of it – and started to ask questions; finally the General Officer Commanding Troops in Egypt (General Jock Burnett Stuart) was asked to go into the matter urgently and to report to the Army Council what was happening. To settle it General Burnett Stuart and my father got into an aeroplane (a less common occurrence than today), and had a meeting at the War Office in London in an endeavour to convince the CIGS that Monty's worth was such that this aberration should be overlooked; but, of course, they had to give an assurance that his ardour in such respects would be curbed in future.

Monty, as I saw him, was a curious mixture. Clearly he was a great and highly dedicated soldier; the sad death of his wife at such a relatively early age seems to have made him even more dedicated. He seemed to me to have reached his zenith at the Battle of El Alamein; I never felt that his success at the landing in Normandy was unqualified – certainly it was marred by controversy with General Eisenhower and the Americans. He set himself up as a religious man and, in many of his 'orders of the day', quoted from the Bible; but his proposal to instal a brothel in Alexandria does not quite fit in with such a reputation. He did not appear to get on well with many of his superiors or indeed his contemporaries – and he had, I think, few true friends. He surrounded himself at his tactical headquarters with a group of young officers who acted as liaison officers or A.D.C.s; perhaps he preferred their company to that of officers more nearly of his age and seniority – and possibly he preferred the company of the young because they would not answer him back. He used these liaison officers to visit front line units and to report on the operational situation to him direct; I met them from time to time whilst with the 1st R. Tanks and, whilst they were generally perfectly pleasant, it was, I thought, a dangerous arrangement which could give the C. in C. a misleading impression if they did not get the situation clear and complete in their minds and report totally accurately on it. In my experience they often did not spend long enough with the regiment they were visiting to do this.

His disloyal attitude to General Eisenhower is well known; but this trait went further. When, in late 1944, my father went to see him at his Headquarters in Brussels, Monty told him in the course of lunch that he had no use whatever for his long-standing Chief of Staff General de Guingand; 'He's mad,' Monty told him. 'Belchem does all my work now.' Brigadier David Belchem, of my Regiment, was his Brigadier General Staff; he was a brilliant, if rather unprincipled, officer but one on whom Monty obviously came to rely. I was waiting outside the house for my father and an American General Claud Thiele, who was travelling with him; my father repeated to me what Monty had said and seemed very surprised. I was too junior to appreciate what was going on but the conversation did come as a shock to me; De Guingand was a very well-known figure and had been his Chief of Staff throughout the desert war too. It was perhaps understandable that Monty might want a change, but it did not seem necessary to tell the world about it.

Monty had been an enormously charismatic leader in the Desert, and he will always have his place in military history for this. When he arrived in Egypt in 1942 he immediately raised the morale of the Army. He made sure that every officer and man knew the situation – what he had to do, and the reason for it; he also made certain that each one of them knew him. Later – after the war – I was speaking to General 'Pip' Roberts who commanded the 22nd Armoured Brigade in 7th Armoured Division at the Battle of El Alamein, and I asked him for his assessment of Monty after he had arrived to take over command of the 8th Army. He said that there was no great difference regarding the planning of the next stage of the North African campaign from that which General Auchinleck had put into effect (General Auchinleck was his predecessor). The difference was that, before Monty's arrival, there was always a 'fall-back' position – perhaps the River Nile or the Suez Canal. After Monty had taken command nothing like this was tolerated; 'We stand and fight at El Alamein,' he said, 'and if we cannot stay there alive, we will stay there dead.' Things were changed and there was clearly going to be no more retreat – and every man knew it.

He was, in short, the leader the nation had been waiting for in those dark wartime days when disaster after disaster was striking our shipping in the Atlantic, when we had lost Singapore and practically the whole of the Far East. The final catastrophe that autumn was the loss of two of our most modern battle cruisers – the *Prince of Wales* and the *Repulse* – in the Far East. Against this background, and also against that of almost continuous retreat since 1940, Monty won the Battle of El Alamein, one of the great battles of modern history and a major turning point in the war.

During this period, whilst he was in North Africa, he had virtually a free hand as commander of the 8th Army. It was when he got to NW Europe with the landing in Normandy and the subsequent advance that he had to work with other allies and commanders; then his weaknesses became more apparent. When he returned to England to take up the post of CIGS at the end of the war, he had not only to work with other people – but also with the government. Few people regarded his tenure at CIGS as a success. Yet CIGS – the professional head of the Army – was the appointment which he must, in his heart, have been aiming for in all his years of service.

Chapter 12

My father

I think it necessary at this stage to say something of my father – his career, personality and relationships; since having reached high rank in the Army, these had a great deal of effect on others, not least on my brother and myself.

Known generally as 'Tim', he was born in Dublin in 1884. He was educated there and in due course, went to the Royal Military Academy at Woolwich (the Shop) and became a Gunner. He fought with distinction as a gunner during the 1914–1918 War and, after this, transferred to the Royal Tank Corps which had just been formed.

In 1914 he became engaged to my mother, and, in the Autumn of that year, they were married. I was born in 1915 and John, my brother, in 1918. After John's birth he effectively parted from my mother, though they were not formally divorced until later. During our schooldays John and I both spent about half of each holiday with my father and half with my mother. My mother was badly off financially and could not afford a proper home, so she lived with her parents who had by then retired to Hove. Since my father had then what amounted to a bachelor establishment, my grandparents' house in Hove became, as I explained earlier in this account, a home for John and myself until my mother married again. Despite her financial circumstances my mother managed to keep in touch with many of the friends that she and my father had made when they were together, and some of these – like my father – rose to high rank in the Army. I saw him only infrequently during the War; much of what follows therefore comes from all my mother told me later from her own experience, from their joint friends with whom she kept in touch, from my contacts in the Army and Navy Club (the Rag) to which I, like many soldiers belonged, and lastly – and at a much later stage – from John.

At the end of the 1914 war my father went on a long course at the school of Army/Air Co-operation at Old Sarum, and after this, to the Staff College as a student. In 1927 he did a year in command of the 3rd Battalion, the Royal Tank Corps. In 1929 he went to the War Office as Assistant Director of Mechanisation. The Director at this time was a Gunner, General Peck.

Both before and after leaving my mother he had come into fairly close association with a number of women, in particular a Mrs. Dod Holmes-Tarn (the wife of a Gunner officer). She was, I believe, very attractive and was certainly wealthy; he became increasingly fond of her. By a strange 'coincidence' Ken Holmes-Tarn (the husband) was also posted to the War Office at the same time. The Holmes-Tarns and he then set up a *'ménage à trois'* by buying – jointly – a largish house called Algars, near Debden Green in Essex.

In the meantime my mother and he had finally decided on a divorce in 1929. The custom of the time, and indeed his own behaviour, would suggest that he should have allowed my mother to divorce him; he would not, however, do this, fearing that it might adversely affect his career. He was extremely ambitious and expected to be appointed an A.D.C. to the King – to which, for some reason he attached much importance. However, because of this and the hurt that it did to my mother, he lost virtually all his old friends but this was not – at any rate at that time – important to him. He must also have known that, after the years of separation, my mother was anxious to marry again whereas, in his case, Dod Holmes-Tarn was not in a position to marry him even if she really wanted to do so; so it was not difficult for him to persuade my mother that the divorce should be arranged the way he wished. Thus my mother concocted a fictitious case of adultery, which would produce the technical grounds for the divorce – which he then obtained.

The *'ménage à trois'* idea seemed splendid to him – and also to Dod (Ken's feelings can only be guessed at). John and I spent half of each school holiday there, but I do not recall that we ever regarded it as home, despite the attractions of a large and rather affluent establishment in the country.

In 1931, possibly frustrated at the poor prospects of ever being able to marry Dod, he met someone else – Hester Phillimore – whilst skiing in Switzerland. She was thirty-one and came from a large and well-known family who owned two big houses, Shedfield and Chilworth Manor – both near Southampton. As well as being well connected, the Phillimores, and their cousins the Willis-Flemings, were an extremely close family. Hester's association with my father undoubtedly gave them some concern; to begin with they were religious, and did not like the idea of her marrying a divorced (however innocently, from a legal point of view) man. Furthermore, he was sixteen years older than her. However, despite the doubts, they became engaged and were married in 1932.

Surprisingly, Dod Holmes-Tarn did not hear the news for some time; I imagine my father found it difficult to tell her. At the time he made less and less plausible excuses (usually 'the General kept me late') for failing to get home in time for the evening meal. Finally, one evening, my father's ex-batman – who had left the army and had become the major-domo of the Algars establishment – came into the drawing-room and, with an entirely straight face, produced for Dod a ball of wool and said, 'Madam, I think the General has left his knitting in the car.' The cat was out of the bag.

After my father and Hester were married they went out to Egypt where he had been appointed to command the Suez Canal Brigade (an infantry brigade) in Moascar Camp, Ismailia. This was an honour for a Gunner turned tank soldier, and he made a great success of it. He showed skill in handling up-and-coming soldiers such as Montgomery and Franklyn, as I have described in the previous chapter. He did, I think, get a reputation at this time for ingenuity and original thinking which stood him in good stead later; and they had a great number of visitors. Altogether he became very well known in the higher echelons of the Army at this period. Whilst they were in Moascar the Holmes-Tarns came from England to stay with them; what exactly happened I do not know, but something certainly did because Hester, the politest and calmest of people, sent them home long before they were due to leave. I later learned from John – who was closer to my father than I was, and who became his A.D.C. for a period during the war, that he had in fact renewed his all too close relationship with Dod Holmes-Tarn.

When he returned home from Egypt in 1936 my father was given commands successively of an Anti-Aircraft Division, an A.A. Corps and finally – just before the outbreak of war – A.A. Command; the latter appointment he held throughout the war. Despite his meteoric rise to high rank he could be appallingly unsound – largely because he insisted in dabbling in matters (particularly if they concerned tanks, on which he considered himself an authority) outside the province of the appointment he held. On one of the few occasions that I saw him during the war I had first-hand evidence of this. I had gone, in 1942, to his home in Flackwell Heath, near Beaconsfield, to spend the night; as one would expect he spoke at length about the war, and he had a lot of papers strewn on the floor –

some of them highly secret (he had little regard for security). He used to have dinner with Winston Churchill frequently to discuss the air defence of the country – though, more often than not, other matters seem to have been discussed as well; he had had one of these dinners the day before my visit.

For some time Stalin had been clamouring publicly – perhaps understandably in view of the casualties being suffered by his armies – for the Allies to open a second front in Europe. My father had convinced himself (probably egged on by Basil Liddell Hart, the military historian, in whom he often confided) that it would be possible successfully to invade the continent of Europe in 1943 if only we disbanded large numbers of infantry units and formed tank armies. These would be landed in France, virtually without any other arms to support them except the R.A.F., and would advance in one enormous thrust through the Netherlands and into Germany. After dealing – doubtless briefly – with A.A. matters, he expounded this idea to Churchill who seized on it and put it to the Chief of the Imperial Staff General (later Field Marshal) Alan Brooke. Even with my very limited experience the whole thing seemed a total fallacy; and, when in 1944 in Normandy, I looked back on this conversation, I viewed the whole idea as incredible. That evening I told my father of my feeling; but he simply dismissed this without arguing the implications of his suggestion – it was good enough for him that Churchill was apparently enthusiastic about it.

Some months later I was with my mother, who had recently seen an old friend who was a senior officer on Alan Brooke's staff. He told her that Alan Brooke had been quite horrified by what was proposed – so indeed were the Army Council – and, a day or two later, he returned to see Churchill and report the Army Council's detailed thoughts and to explain why it was so unsound. When he had concluded Churchill apparently said, 'All right, you can go and I will put Pile in as CIGS.' At this the entire Army Council threatened to resign; and after a good deal of argument, Churchill recanted and no more was heard of the tank army idea. It is not difficult to see why this story found no place in his book *Ack Ack*, though he does hint, in the book, at some rather similar conversation with Lord Beaverbrook.

He was a good, but not a great, soldier; in fairness he never really got a chance to be more as he was never given a field command. He had a good sense of humour, a light touch and got on well with the officers and men he commanded – and the women too, as he started the 'mixed batteries' in A.A. Command; and very successful they were. He never managed to get on with his contemporaries, however, and this failure was made far worse by the manner of his divorce which appalled many of them. At the time of the Suez Crisis in 1956, when I myself was deeply involved in the planning, he asked me one day to have a quick lunch with him at the Rag. It happened to be the day of the funeral of a very well-known and respected Gunner – General Otto Lund – and the club was crammed full of senior Gunners, retired and serving. Amongst them were nearly all of his own contemporaries from the days when he himself was a Gunner. One would have expected my lunch date to have become an occasion for him to meet virtually all of his long-standing friends; instead, not one of them came over to speak to him nor did he say a word to any of them. When I suggested he might like me to leave early (I certainly had plenty to do in the War Office) to give him the chance to talk to them he simply said, 'Oh no – I really can't be bothered.'

John, when he was younger, had a great respect – indeed admiration – for my father. He was less happy with my mother and resented Jock, who was far too strict for him; for me it was the other way round. He had joined the Army at the outbreak of war and was in the Middle East in 1941 and 1942; it was after this that my father made him his A.D.C. At the end of the war he married Katharine Shafe. My father disliked his new daughter-in-law, and made this quite clear to John and, indeed, to everyone else; this cannot have improved their relationship though, for some years, John and he remained on very good terms. Whatever he may have thought, Katharine became a splendid consort to John and an excellent mother to their four happy and successful children.

Very sadly for us, because both John and I were extremely fond of her, Hester died of cancer in 1949. She was a heavy smoker and not very healthy – indeed, both her father and her mother had died when she herself was young. I was still in Germany at this time and, soon after she died, I received a letter from my father enclosing a copy of her will; in this she had left her money to John and myself, with my father having a life interest. We were to be her sole executors. He emphasised that this had, in his view, been done purely for tax reasons; the wording of the will would, he said make no practical difference since we would merely have to sign our agreement to anything he himself decided. At first sight this did seem to make sense; if it had been left without qualification to my father, death duties would have been payable both on her death and on his. The Will, however, appeared to have been hastily drawn up in a number of ways; in particular it provided that if either John or I predeceased him, all the estate was to go to the other – and nothing to the deceased's family. This seemed curious as the Will was made in June 1944 when my expectation of life in Normandy cannot have been all that long; in addition, Hester happened to have been very fond of our (then) only child Fiona, who was three years old when it was written. For many years also John and I wondered why she had decided to re-write her will at all (previously she had presumably left everything to my father) at this particular moment and in such apparent haste. We came to the conclusion, as time went on, that the saving of estate duty was by no means the only reason.

This Will and its implications bedevilled John's and my own relationship with my father thereafter; from the beginning he never consulted us. He often bought and sold shares without a word to us – and then demanded that we sign immediately to put the transaction in order. There was no question of discussion; indeed, on one occasion he tried to insist that we both sign a document giving up our rights and allowing him total authority over the Trust. This, of course, we declined to do.

As I have said earlier, John did – certainly at this time – trust him; I did not. I suppose I was naive to expect him to appreciate my point of view that this was the only money that my family had or were likely to receive, and that Hester had clearly intended it to come to us. And he certainly would never have admitted that both his own father and he had, at times, shown themselves unsound over money matters – though I saw this only too well. So I considered that I owed it to my family to stand firm (using as much tact as I could muster); he remained – I think for the rest of his life – in a state of undisguised fury that he should have been placed under an obligation to discuss anything with anyone.

Very much later I learned from John that my father had had (or perhaps more accurately, had attempted to have) a love affair with a lady to whom John himself had hoped to become engaged – whilst he was still serving in the Middle East; John also told me that, whilst he was my father's A.D.C., he believed that he had – for the third time – renewed his association with Dod Holmes Tarn. We firmly believed that it was likely that Hester had heard of all this, and had consequently changed her Will.

In 1951 he married again – Mollie Home, who was the widow of an Indian Army Brigadier. He was, I think, very happy with Mollie; he had also been happy with Hester, but in a rather different way. Mollie seems to have suited him more than any of his previous wives. The marriage did not, however, do much to keep the family together; apart from anything else, Mollie took a dislike to John (which matched my father's dislike of Katharine) and despised his family. She was an incorrigible snob, and this trait guided all her relationships. Her side of the family fell apart too as, soon after the wedding, her only daughter got divorced from Hal Hudson, an excellent chap who subsequently became Chairman of Lloyds. Relations between my father and myself – and increasingly with John too – became steadily worse until after 1961, neither of us saw him again.

He had few real friends, and by the time he died – just after my mother in 1976 – he had been drawn closer and closer to Mollie's family; Mollie herself, her daughter Elizabeth and her son-in-law Roger were all he really had.

One final thought about my father has occurred to me over the years. He was always very aggrieved that officers and men of A.A. Command were not awarded any special decoration at the end of the war. I know nothing of the merits of their case but have often wondered if, had his relationships with his contemporaries been a little more cordial, the outcome of this argument might not have been more favourable to him – and to his Command. After all, politicians come and go, as indeed Winston Churchill (who might well have been prevailed upon to do something to help if he had remained in power) did; but your professional colleagues remain and they might – in the long run – be of more use to you than your political master. My father, however, never thought this.

Chapter 13

The War Office and three years in England

After the death of my stepmother my father seemed very broken. He had been asking me for some time to try and return home for a spell; but, apart from one short visit to see Hester in hospital, I did not feel I could reasonably ask to be released at that moment as a new Chief of Staff, General Tuck, had just arrived and was taking over at Rhine Army Headquarters. However, after he had been in the saddle for six months, both Pam and I thought we should now make the effort to leave Germany; so I decided to discuss the matter with him. I did this with a good deal of personal regret as, after two years in the Chief of Staff's office, I had really learned the ropes – and I knew both the Commander in Chief and the Chief of Staff and liked them both. Furthermore, there were a few side perks which appealed to me greatly. Every Saturday in winter I ran the Chief of Staff's shoot which was a most pleasant task; he selected his guests from the more senior – or more frequently the more amusing – members of the staff and they, and their wives, came out with us for the day. We usually got extremely good bags of partridge and pheasant as there had not been much shooting there (of that sort) during the previous six years. It was always a very pleasant day and a marvellous relaxation from the intensive workload we all had during the week. I also took to fishing; the River Diemal, not far from Bad Oeynhausen, was one of the best trout streams in Germany and, since General Tuck was a highly experienced fisherman, I learned a lot from him. I have never lost my love for this sport. I was not, however, to be 'released' for another six months.

We also had particularly good relations with our Allies in the other Zones of Germany, and this led to some pleasant social contacts. This had been true of the Americans from the time we landed in Normandy, but General

58

Tuck had taken a special interest in developing an equally good rapport with the French. Amongst other things he organised a series of tennis matches to be played alternately in Baden Baden (the French Army Headquarters) and at Bad Oeynhausen. To get to Baden Baden we were allowed to use the Commander in Chief's train, on which we travelled in the utmost luxury with comfortable sleepers, a drawing room, dining room and a bar – and in very cheerful company. This was a splendid start to our visit and, of course, when we got to our destination, tennis became only a relatively small part of the programme – it was one long party, and we all certainly got to know the French.

One day in March 1950, I was walking with General Tuck across the park to his house when he turned to me and said that he had spoken to the Commander in Chief about my future, and that they both felt I should go home in June. They were going to arrange a posting for me to the War Office as they thought I should learn more of the 'higher direction of the Army'. In June therefore I duly returned home, with my family, to take up the appointment of G.S.O. 2 (2nd Grade Staff Officer) in the War Office general staff manpower branch known as S.D.4 (S.D. stood for 'staff duties').

We immediately set about the task of finding a house to rent – no easy matter in those days around London. We certainly could not afford to buy one as our combined assets at that time amounted only to £800 in Savings Certificates, most of which was my gratuity from the war. Eventually we found a flat in Cheam – the top floor of an old house in an out of the way country lane known as Peaches Close. It was near the station which was a great help to me, and we liked it; we particularly liked the garden which was large and totally wild and neglected. It had obviously been a lovely spot and we approached with joy the job of clearing the garden, and restoring something of its former charm. The owners had given us a completely free hand over all this, and let us regard the garden as our own.

Nearby, and in a vastly more expensive house, lived a Mr. Harry Clayton and his family (he, his wife, a boy and a girl; there was also an elder girl, but she had married and left home). Harry was chairman of the firm 'Cementation', now part of the Trafalgar House group of companies; indeed, for many years, he virtually was the firm. He had joined it during the First World War when it was very small and in a bad way, and had devoted his life to reviving it and to its development as one of the foremost construction firms in the country. My father joined it at the end of 1946. Harry Clayton told me one day, whilst we were playing golf together, how he had managed to build up the company technically, but that he felt at the end of the war that it was necessary to 'put it on the map'; he thought that the addition of my father's name to the Company note paper heading would achieve this – as he had become so well known during the war. He and his family could not have been kinder to us; we only had to have a bout of 'flu (for some reason we all seemed to get these things at the same time, which temporarily hampered our housekeeping) and they would both be round – immediately and frequently – with cooked food and every kind of offer to help. We saw a lot of this family during our three years in Cheam; sadly, just as we were leaving Harry Clayton died, and his wife died soon afterwards. Over the years we have maintained touch with his two surviving children, Colin and Barbara. Barbara has since married – Ernest Blomfield – and now lives in a house in Cheam on almost the same site as that in which we lived in 1950.

It was whilst we were in this house in Cheam in 1951 that Vanessa was born in Queen Charlotte's Hospital.

Whilst at the War Office I was very busy as manpower is one of the most sensitive subjects in all the three service ministries – it is something we are always desperately short of. I had to service one Army Council sub-committee which met once a fortnight, and produce agenda and minutes – and to follow up all the decisions that stemmed from it. I also had to keep day-to-day control of the availability of manpower in all branches of the Army, and to keep my Colonel and other superior officers informed as to how their policy decisions were being implemented. To anyone visiting the War Office it seems a most leisurely place, but this is misleading; it takes a service officer about nine months to get into almost any job and to learn the ways of civil servants (it is, after all, a civil ministry). As you learn so you appreciate that practically every action you take, or letter you write, concerns numerous other branches – and perhaps services. The standard of work is extremely high, and any shortfall in this respect rapidly becomes known to innumerable other people and rebounds on oneself. I seldom left the office before 6.30 p.m., even on normal days; when there were meetings it could often be 8.00 p.m. or later before one was free. So our social life as a family was confined to weekends; these were normally free of work except that I had to do duty for the directorate (of Staff Duties) one Saturday morning each month. We were given a free hand over the time we took for lunch; nominally we were allowed an hour but, if we were busy, we might go out for ten minutes and get a sandwich. On other occasions one took longer, and I would then lunch at the Rag (or perhaps somewhere else with a friend). In this way I met a lot of people in other walks of life in London – particularly in the City. From time to time I lunched with Hal Hudson

(Mollie's ex-son-in-law) with whom I got on extremely well. Talking to him and to other friends I started being interested in finance; through one of them I met a Mr. Middleton of a firm called 'Investment Registry' in Grafton Street. It was run by a man, then relatively little known outside the City, called Charles Clore.

In my spare time from manpower problems I started thinking about our own family finances, which were pretty sparse. It was clear that our £800 nest egg was far too small to be of much use in these inflationary days; and that, even if we lost all or some of it, this would not be an unmitigated disaster. So we placed half this money in a firm called Sears (not surprisingly, recommended by Investment Registry since Charles Clore was also Chairman of Sears) and the other half in a wild speculation which Investment Registry also suggested to me – the White Pass and Yukon railway in Northern Canada. What persuaded me to be so unnaturally incautious I cannot think; I must have imagined that, having been sent to learn about the 'higher direction of the Army', I would have an assured future and a secure salary to boot! Anyhow, by a miracle and after a shaky start both did well – particularly the White Pass and Yukon which climbed sharply in price to about five times its original cost, when I lost my nerve and sold it; I kept the Sears shares for many years, and an excellent investment they proved to be. I also kept my association with Investment Registry until, many years later, they were taken over by a much larger organisation. Thanks to this start and to the very good advice I was given during the next few years, our finances had, by the time I was due to leave the Army, become less parlous.

After my tour of duty at the War Office I was sent on a course at the Joint Services Staff College at Latimer, Buckinghamshire. This was an interesting six months' course intended to be an intermediate training between the Camberley Staff College and the Imperial Defence College. There were lectures from various eminent people both from within and from outside the services. These were particularly valuable as we took it in turns to have lunch or dinner afterwards with the speaker, which gave us an excellent chance to get to know him better and to question him more intimately. Two such speakers whose words I well remember were the then chairman of the Burma Oil Company who told me (in 1953) categorically that there was no chance whatever of oil being discovered in or near this country! Four years later, when I arrived in Washington, I was given a briefing in the Pentagon during which I was told that oil had in fact just been discovered – almost underneath the offices of the Royal Dutch Shell Company in Holland! This was the start of the exploration which led to the development shortly afterwards of the great North Sea oil fields. It does sometimes go to show that even the great experts can be wrong sometimes. The other memorable lecturer was Douglas Hyde, author of the book *I Believed*; a communist turned Roman Catholic, having totally disavowed communism. He taught me more about communism, its methods and its dangers, that day than I have ever managed to learn from any other source.

Chapter 14

Korea and the Canal Zone of Egypt

In the summer of 1953 I went out to Korea to join the 1st Royal Tanks who had already been there for six months, during which time I was on my course at Latimer. I went by sea in the S.S. *Asturias*, a pleasant but rather long (four weeks) voyage. Hostilities had just ceased and we were concentrated in an area some five miles behind the front line in case the armistice should break down. This did not happen, however, and our chief problem became one of boredom. Korea was a desolate country and, at that time, very poor; It is very hot indeed in summer and unbelievably cold in winter. I lived in a caravan but, despite this, the boiling water brought to me for shaving each morning frequently froze before I could get my brush to it during the winter. Seoul, the capital of South Korea, was then a very dirty and unkempt town, and one to be avoided if possible.

In addition to being a rather inhospitable country, life was not made easier by the fact that there were still minefields everywhere; it was obviously going to take a considerable time to clear them all. The only recreation worth while was pheasant shooting. This must have been the best anywhere; the birds were magnificent – and enormous. Some of us went out most afternoons to shoot for the pot – hoping to avoid stepping into a minefield as we did so; our mess lived almost exclusively on pheasant.

It is interesting that this poor and desolate country has now the fastest economic growth rate in the world; and that Seoul, which we all regarded with such contempt in 1953, now has a population of over ten million, is larger than London; it has its own international airport, luxury hotels, first-rate shops and is a thriving modern society.

The Regiment left Korea in January 1954, in the *Empire Orwell* troopship, bound for Egypt and a year's service in the Canal Zone. Here we took over from the 5th Royal Inniskilling Dragoon Guards in the camp at Shandur, on the edge of the Great Bitter Lake. Shandur was some

63

twenty-five miles south of Moascar – the camp where my father had his Brigade headquarters twenty years previously, and where I stayed with them on two occasions whilst on leave from Sandhurst. It was, I need hardly say, far less comfortable. There was considerable anti-British feeling on the part of the Egyptians who realised that it was only a matter of a short time before the British Army would leave Egypt altogether. There were continual incidents caused by Egyptians sniping at people (whether in uniform or not) travelling on the road which runs alongside the Canal. As a result all vehicles were under orders to move only in pairs, one of which had to carry a loaded machine gun; there was no doubt that, if a vehicle broke down, it was in danger – thus every journey by the troops or military individuals had to be accounted for. No one was allowed to leave the camp, which itself was surrounded by coils of barbed wire and heavily guarded, without permission. For recreation there were rudimentary sporting facilities within the camp area; we did, however, also take parties of soldiers and, when they were able to join us, families, to swim in the Suez Canal nearby. This was very popular, particularly because large ships were continually passing through and the wash which resulted gave the swimmer the thrill of gliding on a large and rapidly moving wave back to the shore. Needless to say, these swimming parties had to be guarded – machine gun posts being placed around.

We were told that the Regiment would be in the Canal Zone for about eighteen months and, since many officers and men had already been abroad without their families for a year – in Korea – we felt that we should make an effort to bring some families out from England. Hitherto this had been expressly forbidden but we were fairly confident that, if allowed to do so, we could improvise the necessary accommodation using only our own resources. There were a number of disused army huts in the camp area but unfortunately only three buildings which even remotely resembled a house. However, the huts were in fair condition and, since National Service was still in force, we had in the Regiment quite a large number of bricklayers and plumbers. We also saw one other aid to our plans; there was such a dearth of accommodation in the area that those people who did find something – mostly near Ismailia – and who got permission to bring out their families, were given an enormous financial allowance. This amounted to near double the scale normally granted, and seems to have been authorised only because every stick of furniture had to be brought from outside Egypt and this was, of course, very expensive. We thought that, if we could get a loan to make possible the start of our building programme (i.e. to buy bricks, etc.), we could probably arrange to repay this by 'taxing' the individuals who occupied the houses – since they would then be in receipt of the enhanced allowance. It meant that they would probably have insufficient money to purchase all the furniture they required, but this would have to be accepted.

We put our proposals to Army H.Q., but were firmly told that on no account would we be allowed to build houses by these means and that, anyhow, this was a predominantly 'non-married' station and that we should have realised this. However, by a stroke of luck, the Commander in Chief of the Middle East Command at that time was none other than my old master – General Charles Keightley who, of course, I knew well. He had heard that I had arrived with the 1st Royal Tanks as Second-in-Command and, after a week or two, kindly asked me to dinner. Before going I discussed with my commanding officer, Lt. Colonel N.E.O. (Edward) Watts, O.B.E., the idea of my mentioning our problem to the C. in C.; he said he would welcome this. I found Charles Keightley as friendly and hospitable as he had been in Germany, and he wanted to know all about the Regiment and how we were settling in; so amongst other things I mentioned our proposal to house some of our families. He was extremely receptive and turned to his chief administrative officer, General Willie Cole, who was also at the dinner (and incidentally who was the very officer who had turned down our formal request) and asked him to make it possible for us to do what we had asked as he thoroughly approved of the idea. As I said goodbye to him at the end of the evening he asked me to ensure that he was told when the first batch of families was due to arrive, as he wished to come and visit them.

So we set about building the houses in our spare time, till we had accommodation for about twenty-five families – approximately the number who had expressed a desire to come out to Egypt, at that stage.

Our time at Shandur was not just house-building, however; we did a great deal of training in the desert, mostly astride the road from Suez to Cairo, an area which the tank crews got to know intimately – just as a previous generation of tank crewmen in the Regiment had got to know the Western Desert twenty years earlier. It was not that there was any real threat to our security on the Canal, except from snipers who could not be described as more than a nuisance: but, since all the Egyptian Army units were in or near Cairo, the Suez road was one of the only two routes they could use if they did decide to interfere with our occupation of the Canal Zone.

I should at this stage mention the Adjutant of the Regiment, Captain (later Colonel) Alan Parks. He had been with us almost continuously since he joined the Regiment in Normandy; he had a splendid war record and had since proved his worth in peace. He well deserved to be appointed Adjutant,

and was a tower of strength in coping with the rather rugged conditions of
the Canal Zone. A few years later, when I became Commandant of the
Tank Driving and Maintenance School at Bovington, he was promoted
Major and became my senior instructor – a duty he carried out with his
usual efficiency and cheerfulness.

There were also duties to be done outside those of regimental training;
one which came my way was a mission to Iraq. The Government was
anxious to sell Centurion tanks to the Iraqis and, since the 1st Royal Tanks
was the only armoured regiment in Egypt, and was equipped with Cen-
turions, we were told to take on the duty of salesmen. It was decided that we
should send two troops – each of four tanks – overland on transporters to
Habbaniya near Baghdad. They were to go via Aquaba, a distance of some
950 miles, much of it on unmade roads and tracks; it was planned to
complete the journey in six days. I had been told that I was to take charge of
the operation and was sent for to meet the Army Commander (General,
later Field Marshal, Sir Richard Hull) in Moascar to be 'briefed'. He told
me that I was to fly to Habbaniya and to arrive ahead of the tank convoy to
give me time to meet the Iraqi Defence Minister and to make arrangements
for demonstrating the tanks. After receiving my instructions I drove back to
Shandur and arranged for the two troops, together with some ten administrative vehicles carrying rations, fuel and fitters, to start off in three days. I
saw the party on its way and then took my aircraft so that I arrived in
Habbaniya well in advance.

I was met by our Military Attaché who took me to the R.A.F. officers'
mess where it had been arranged for me to stay (Habbaniya was an
enormous R.A.F. staging airfield): he told me that an appointment had been
made for me to meet the Minister of Defence in two days, and that he would
drive me to Baghdad the following day. In the meantime I had a few hours
to reconnoitre the area and make a provisional plan for the demonstration
of the tanks when they arrived.

The road to Baghdad from Habbaniya (some fifty miles) was atrocious;
we travelled in the Attaché's four wheel drive jeep, but there were large
potholes all the way, and, in some parts, sheer drops of two or three feet
right across the road. Altogether the journey took us over three hours, and I
was glad to arrive at the Attaché's house and have a few hours' peace – and
a short walk round Baghdad.

The following day I was taken to the Ministry of Defence and explained
to the Minister and his staff my proposed arrangements for the demonstration. He agreed with these in principle but decided that he would like to
look at it on the ground. So I spent a second night in the Attaché's house

and, the following day, the Minister and I flew back to Habbaniya in a small aircraft – a more pleasant and certainly a quicker trip than the outward one by road. After walking round the area for most of the rest of that day the Minister approved the plan I had outlined and also confirmed that we would be able to fire live ammunition.

A day or two later, the two tank troops arrived, and, though the crews were tired, the tanks seemed in reasonably good order; we soon got down to rehearsing the demonstration which the Minister had asked should take place in ten days.

On the appointed day a surprisingly large crowd appeared; the Minister, who had a place of honour on a raised platform which the R.A.F. had kindly made for us, had apparently brought most of his Ministry, and there were detachments from Iraqi armoured units from all over the country. Fortunately it was all a success: no tanks broke down and, when the two troops opened fire, it did look impressive – the targets being blown to bits in a matter of seconds. I later learned that the Iraqi government had placed an order for a considerable number of Centurion tanks (they probably made good use of them in the recent Iran/Iraq War!).

I stayed on with my detachment in Habbaniya for a month to start setting up a training organisation for Iraqi officers and N.C.O.s, and then handed over to Major Charles Armitage, M.C., of the Queen's Bays who had been sent out to relieve me – so I could resume my duties as second-in-command of the 1st Royal Tanks.

It was during the eighteen months that the Regiment spent in the Canal Zone that the El Alamein War Memorial was opened by Field Marshal Montgomery. Since I knew our Military Attaché in Cairo – Hugh Fraser, an old friend with whom I had served on and off since we were subalterns together before the war – we managed to get tickets. My Commanding Officer and his wife (Edward and Joy Watts) and, of course, Pam came with me. It was a memorable day from every point of view; but the many names of good comrades – both officers and men – whose names were inscribed on the memorial made it rather a sad one for me.

There was, however, an interesting sequel because afterwards we were invited to a party at Burgh el Arab, where Monty had established his H.Q. just before the battle. There were a quite surprising number of British people and their families living in Burgh el Arab, and who had done so continuously since prewar days. They told us that they were there during the battle of El Alamein and that the gunfire was deafening, although they were thirty miles away. What they all did during the war years I never discovered, but they were a pleasant lot and they gave us a great party.

In the spring of 1955 I returned home – to take command of the Leeds Rifles. In many ways this was a most pleasant command although I would have preferred command of a regular regiment. Command of the Leeds Rifles did, however, have much to commend it; it was a fully equipped armoured regiment and a very strong one – over 900 fully trained men as we still had National Service. In addition I got to know many of the people in and around Leeds due to the help given to me by our Regimental Colonel, Noel Tetley (Chairman of the well-known brewery). Because of his kindness I soon found myself a member of the Leeds Club (unusual for an 'outsider') and invitations flowed to us from all kinds of people and organisations. Included in these was one from the Lord Mayor to come to dinner and meet H.R.H. the Duke of Edinburgh, who was visiting a hospital and two factories in Leeds – and a very interesting evening it was.

Unfortunately this pleasant command was interrupted by the onset of the Suez crisis of 1956.

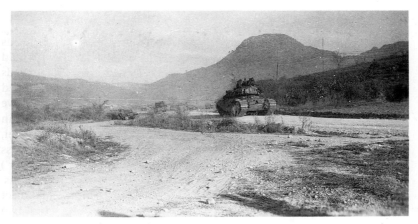

Centurion tank moving up to the front in Korea. 1953.

Pamela, digging a desert garden in Egypt. 1954.

Vanessa cleaning the tank park.

Pamela, Fiona and Vanessa at the de Lesseps statue. Port Said.

The Officers HQ 2nd Corps in Port Said 1956. Front Row: Brig. Tucker, Brig. Wainwright, Col. Aubert, Brig. Darling, Gen. Stockwell, Brig. Lacey, Mr. Tom Bromley, Brig. Henniker, Col. Evans. Second Row: Col. Stubbs, Col. Bloxham, Brig. Officer, Grp. Capt. Graham, Col. Gillman, Brig. Saunders. Col Burkin, Wing Cdr. Jannaway, Maj. Mike Hunt. Just behind: Maj. Cornforth, The Author, Maj. Shepherd.

Leeds Rifles Annual Camp. General's visit – with General Sir Geoffrey Evans, KBE., CB., DSO. and Major Richard Tetley, the Squadron Leader.

Christmas at 'San Francisco' Louisiana. 1959.

Pamela with 17th century mitre cap – from Caspar, Wyoming. 1960.

Marriage of Vanessa to Rory Mackean, February 1972.

Marriage of Fiona to Mark Towse, October 1976.

*Josephine and our joint grandchildren –
Cressida, Charlotte and Virginia*

Honeymoon in Venice.

Dinner at the Mansion House, London 1984 – Josephine and Myself.

Chapter 15

The Suez Operation – 1956

During the summer of 1956 the newspapers were increasingly full of the growing crisis in the Middle East. President Nasser of Egypt got more confident – indeed truculent – daily. He did, however, have one weakness; he desperately wanted to build a new high dam in Upper Egypt and he hoped and expected this to be financed by United States and British money. One day, when Nasser was being highly uncooperative over the maintenance of international control of the Suez Canal, the U.S. Secretary of State – Foster Dulles – suddenly withdrew his country's offer of a contribution towards the building of the dam. At this Nasser, who was clearly being aided and abetted by Russia, announced that he was 'nationalising' the Suez Canal – and that the Russians would give him the money to build the dam. The crisis got worse and there was talk of intervention by the West to secure the free passage of all ships through the Canal.

I was sitting in my office in Leeds in late July 1956 when the telephone rang; a chap I knew well in the Military Secretary's department of the War Office told me that I was to hand over my command immediately to my second-in-command, come to London and be prepared to fly to the Middle East at short notice. He added a bit of private advice to me 'Don't miss this on any account.' So I left my long-suffering family to pack up our house in Leeds and to move themselves to Pam's father's house in Newbury (her mother had died the previous year); I took the first available train to London. I arranged to stay temporarily at the Rag, and deposited my suitcase there before walking to Whitehall. It was a Saturday afternoon and I got to the War Office about 4.00 p.m. expecting to find most people away for the weekend. However, it was a veritable hive of activity and, as soon as I had arrived, I was grabbed by someone I did not know – but who seemed to know me; he took me down to the basement which had been used by the

69

government during the war as an operations room during the bombing. It was an enormous labyrinth of corridors and rooms and, as we walked through it, there did not seem to be another soul about; unsurprisingly, because there was not. My colleague told me that he was acting for the Director of Military Operations who was sponsoring the headquarters being assembled; he added that I was the only person to have arrived so far and that I was to be the G.S.O.1 (First Grade General Staff Officer) of a Corps to be known as 2nd Corps, which was being formed for the purpose of planning an operation to reoccupy the Suez Canal. I could not help reflecting that we had only left the Suez Canal Zone about nine months earlier, and that it would have been a good deal easier if we had remained there.

After about an hour I heard footsteps and walked along a passage to meet the new arrival; he told me that he was Brigadier (later General Sir Kenneth) Darling, and that he was to be the Chief of Staff. He had already been to the Cabinet Offices and had learned that we were going to be required to produce a plan for the approval of the Cabinet by Tuesday morning. In my innocence I had always thought that the War Office had plans for any eventuality – anywhere; even more was I sure they would have plans for Egypt since we had been in occupation of the Canal so recently. I could not have been more mistaken; apart from the Port Said airfield (Gamil) about which there was information we had far more questions than there appeared to be answers within the War Office.

So we set to work with the scanty information we were able to obtain and continued to work throughout the night. Our respective trains of thought were peppered by a stream of new arrivals who had come to join the H.Q.; these I had to put in the offices we had provisionally earmarked for them and tell them their jobs. Together we produced – as students at the Staff Colleges are trained to do – an 'appreciation of the situation' and a plan. The following evening the Corps Commander, General Hugh Stockwell, arrived and approved the document we had written – with a few amendments. By midday Monday we had collected a staff of 120 officers, including contingents from the Royal Navy and the Royal Air Force. A few days later we were joined by a French staff; by now we were a substantial headquarters, representing all the services, both French and our own. The operation on which we were engaged was, we were informed, to be called 'Musketeer'.

Our first plan was returned to us by the Cabinet with a mass of queries and comments; the latter we incorporated in an amended plan which became a truly massive document. The plan did not appear to us – nor, I believe, to the Government – wholly satisfactory, and we set about revising it. I don't think I have ever worked harder, even during the War; I remember many nights without sleep at all, and there were virtually none when I left the War Office before 2.00 a.m. in the early stages of planning. We had to be back in the Office by 8.30 a.m. because, as the days went on, we found ourselves increasingly in command of troops, as well as being a planning headquarters. Not only were the hours long, but we worked underground with an artificial air system and this became tiring after a time. So little did we know of what was happening outside the building that a large blackboard was obtained by the porter at the entrance; on this he chalked up the prevailing weather – so that we knew whether or not to take umbrellas if we had to leave the place for any reason. One of the minor domestic difficulties was finding somewhere to live, since we had no idea whatever how long we would remain in London. I, like one or two others, was all right in the Rag for a few days; but the Club were unused to our 'unsocial hours' and they clearly hoped we would all find somewhere else before long. Eventually I found a one-room flat in Lowndes Square at which I could keep what hours I found necessary – and I was able to get out on the basis of one week's notice.

Every day at 2.00 p.m. I represented the Corps Headquarters at a meeting of all the main War Office Directors (some forty major generals). These were frustrating and tedious meetings with long discussions on every detailed aspect of our preparations, and they frequently went on until late afternoon or evening; but, tedious or not, they were clearly necessary as the operation was becoming very complicated indeed – bedevilled as it was with politics. There were, however, some amusing moments. One subject which recurred was the waterproofing of the tanks earmarked as part of the initial assault; it was thought that the landing craft might have to put them ashore in some four to five feet of water. The Director of the Royal Armoured Corps, General 'Fairy' Foote, V.C. – a very gallant, pleasant, chubby-faced rather than a brilliant man – referred to this matter persistently and at such length that there was a noticeable groan from around the table when it became his turn to speak. On one such occasion, at the end of the meeting, I was speaking to Colonel Ken Hunt (the War Office staff officer responsible for servicing the meeting) who showed me a note which he had picked up after the directors had departed; it had been passed from the Engineer in Chief (General Robby Ewbank) – an officer with an unbounded sense of humour – to a colleague as General Foote was speaking. It read, 'The DRAC himself needs waterproofing; he has been out of his depth ever since Operation Musketeer started!'

Before we left London for Cyprus at the end of October we had produced over twenty plans, or variations of plans, for the approval of the Cabinet. The best, from a purely military point of view, involved a landing at Alexandria by sea in support of the Parachute Brigades which would land in the desert between Alexandria and Cairo. If Cairo could have been taken by a quick stroke such as we envisaged, the Suez Canal would have fallen into our hands. This would obviate the difficulty and possible danger of confining our advance to the narrow (fifty-mile) causeway from Port Said to Ismailia, over which the advance was bound to be slow and easily blocked by the enemy. This plan was, however, sharply dismissed and we were told to restrict our planning to a landing at Port Said. Here there was only scope for a small British airborne landing (just to secure the airfield), and the main thrust of the assault would have to be seaborne. This was further complicated by the fact that, since there is no anchorage deep enough for the assault ships in Cyprus, the whole force would have to be based on Malta which was six days' steaming time from Port Said. So we had in effect to tell the Prime Minister that he must think up his *casus belli* for the invasion six days before anything could happen on the ground. This is, of course, a situation no politician likes and, as a result, we were told to think again. Our re-think gave rise to the possibility of an intensive bombing programme. This would make possible an immediate reaction if Nasser would not accede to any ultimatum we might give – that he should withdraw his forces from the Canal area at once. The R.A.F. proposed to bomb the Egyptian airfields and Cairo Radio and considered that the destruction would be such that the Army would be able to land 'with their brief cases'. But the effect of this bombing internationally and in the United Nations – and above all in the U.S.A. – was devastating. The French were seething that the Alexandria plan should have been vetoed by the British Government; they regarded it as far the best approach – so, in our hearts, did we. The French clearly felt that we were not only perfidious but – worse still – stupid.

The Prime Minister was obviously worried, when discarding this Alexandria plan, that he could not state his real reason – that it was not possible politically to allow any extension of the fighting from the Canal itself; in his view our plan would have looked even more like naked aggression, whereas the Port Said landing could be put over as an attempt to divide the Israeli and Egyptian forces and thus safeguard the Canal for international use. The comment he wrote on the front page of the draft we had submitted was, 'You are well aware of your instructions – to plan a landing and reoccupation of the Suez Canal; you should bear in mind the need to do this incurring few casualties and of inflicting the minimum on the enemy.'

One other problem presented itself in the course of planning: that of drinking water. Egypt was extremely short of water; its main source came from the 'sweet water' canal which ran parallel with, and along the length of, the Suez Canal. It would, we thought, be easy for the Egyptians to deny us this source and we therefore had to include in our plans provision for bringing in a large amount of water from outside the country. To this end I was deputed to form a committee to ascertain how much was needed and how it could best be transported. The result was a most detailed study which took about a week to prepare.

I flew out to Cyprus on my own, two days after the H.Q. had left, having remained behind to assist the R.A.F. with their targetting for the bombing. I eventually left from Lyneham Airfield in Wiltshire, seen off by Pam and by the Station Commander – Dicky Abrahams, an old friend from my days at Latimer. Just before taking off I was given a message that General Daunt (the General Officer commanding troops in Malta) wanted to see me, and that arrangements had been made for my plane to land in Malta in the evening so that I could see him. I had no idea what he wanted to ask so I ensured that I had, in my bag, all the latest plans, movement tables and orders so that (I hoped) I could answer his questions. I arrived in his office very late, as the flight had been slower than expected, to be given a message that the General had gone to bed – 'Would I please return in the morning at 9.00 a.m.' So I found a place to spend the night and arranged for the plane to be delayed overnight. As I had some spare time that evening I decided to go and see the 6th Royal Tanks who were in Malta and were going to be in the assault. They were commanded by one Tom Gibbon, whom I knew extremely well as we had joined the Regiment together from Sandhurst; he had lost an arm during the war, but he, and indeed the whole Regiment, seemed in very good spirits that evening.

At 9.00 a.m. I appeared in the General's office and, after a brief word of welcome and thanks, he saw that I had a brief case full of plans and other documents and said, 'You can put all that paper away – I only want to ask you one thing; why are you doing it?' I later learned that he was an intensely religious man and that he was clearly greatly disturbed about the operation, preparations for which were, of course, going on in his own command. I said that I honestly felt he should be addressing his question to someone far higher than me; and that as far as I myself was concerned I believed we were doing what the Government had told us to do. To this he replied that he considered it a wholly immoral operation (which it may have been) and that the troops would resent having to do it (which they certainly did not). He

added that, at the very least, General Stockwell should issue an Order of the
Day telling the troops why the operation was to take place. He gave me to
understand that he had evidence of reluctance, on the part of some units, to
take part; so I mentioned to him that I had been able to visit the 6th Royal
Tanks the previous evening and that this was certainly not the case with
them – rather an eagerness to have a go. The British Army had spent many
years in Egypt and, though it was a popular station, the Egyptians
themselves had never been much liked or respected. I said goodbye and got
in my car to return to the airfield; on the way I thought that General Daunt
must have greatly regretted having gone to bed early the previous day – thus
giving me the opportunity to wander round his troops and doubtless spread
what he must have considered heresy! Anyway, I would be able to assure
General Stockwell that at least the 6th Royal Tanks were in good heart, and
I knew that would please him. I landed at Akrotiri Airfield in Cyprus that
afternoon, went straight to General Stockwell's office and told him what
General Daunt had said to me. He rounded on me – as if to blow up – and
said 'He's a bloody fool; what the hell can I say? You go and write the . . .
order yourself, Freddy, and I'll sign it if you think it will please him.'
General Stockwell always called a spade a spade, and we all knew exactly
where we were with him; he never let any of his staff down and, though he
may have made his mistakes, he was a splendid man to serve. His morals,
like mine, were simple. Quite honestly none of us knew enough of the
politics and deeper purpose of the operation to be sure as to whether it was
immoral or not. In the whole time I was involved in its planning I only met
one man – out of all the large numbers of officers and men from all three
services – who expressed any reluctance to take part. Our job was surely to
carry out the purpose of our government as efficiently as possible; it was as
simple as that.

The military plan went exactly as intended. The bombing programme
effectively knocked out the Egyptian airfields – and therefore their air force
– and also Cairo Radio. The Parachute Brigade secured Gamil Airfield for
our own use and the Royal Marine Commando came in in helicopters (the
first time they had ever been used in an assault); the leading troops of the
3rd Division had already put to sea when the bombing started and they –
with the 6th Royal Tanks – were therefore not far behind. By the end of the
first afternoon we had the town of Port Said firmly in our hands, and a
small mixed force of tanks and infantry then started moving rapidly south
towards Ismailia; it was clear, from the B.B.C. radio broadcasts, that we
could be stopped at any moment. In the event the leading units got to El

Cap, about thirty-two miles from Port Said, before we received a direct order from the War Office to cease operations.

We spent two months in Port Said and, during this period, the offices of the Suez Canal Company became our headquarters. Our set-up was very top-heavy as we were, by then, a large corps headquarters geared to control several divisions in battle. Owing to the fact that we were unable to move off the causeway to the right or left, all that the Corps H.Q. effectively controlled operationally was the one infantry company at El Cap. So, in addition to facing the Egyptians, this overworked company had to face numerous visits from frustrated commanders and staff officers who had nothing else to do. As we were all virtually unemployed, that two months seemed an age. At last, just before Christmas, we were relieved by a United Nations force and we re-embarked. I left on the last ship (the S.S. *Asturias*, in which I had three years previously sailed to Korea); just before doing so the Deputy Provost Marshal (Commander of the Military Police) and I lowered the flag – for the last time on Egyptian territory.

Chapter 16

A tour of duty at the Pentagon

When I arrived in England I was told that I was to go to Washington D.C. in six months, as head of our Army intelligence team and that, in the meantime, I had better learn something about intelligence. So we rented a flat for the period in order to be within easy reach of London. In July 1957, armed with six months' worth of intelligence briefings from numerous departments in Whitehall – and a course at the Army School of Intelligence at Maresfield in Sussex – we set sail. Fiona was at boarding school and we arranged for her to join us in the holidays; but Pam, Vanessa and I embarked in the S.S. *Queen Elizabeth* (first class) for New York. We arrived early in the day and, as we approached, saw one of the world's most unforgettable sights – the Manhattan skyline at sunrise. From New York we took the train for Washington where we were met by a large detachment from the British Joint Services Mission, one or two of whom kindly escorted us to the flat we had taken, just off Wisconsin Avenue. We thought that a flat (apartment) would suit us better than a house as we wanted to travel as much as possible.

My job was a new one; we had a number of staff officers in the Pentagon at 'desks' with their U.S. opposite numbers. I was instructed to weld this staff into a unit and to co-ordinate its work; and I was to endeavour to become sufficiently acceptable – and indeed useful – to the Americans to persuade them to provide me with an office in the Pentagon. The argument for this was that the senior U.S. Army Intelligence Officer in London had an office in the War Office.

I had never realised, until I arrived in Washington, that the Pentagon was then a public building. It had shops, banks and many cafeterias and coffee shops; any member of the public could go in and make use of these, provided he could get there. There was no public transport to the building, which is surrounded by many acres of car parks whose spaces were all

76

individually allocated. If, however, you could manage to get a lift from someone entitled to a space, there was nothing to stop you spending the day there, doing your shopping and having lunch. As a result of this, security had to be particularly strict. There were various barriers, heavily guarded, where only those with especial security clearances could pass; and any breach of security was punished with extreme severity, the officer or enlisted man concerned having his record of service permanently endorsed, which seriously affected his future. Much of this has been changed, however, during the last thirty years; the Washington Metro – which was not built in 1960 – now has a station at the Pentagon. Furthermore, perhaps because of this, the public access to the building, though still allowed, is greatly curtailed.

My routine was militarily very unorthodox. After dealing with my morning mail in my own office – in a building known as the 'Main Navy', about a mile from the Pentagon – I would go by a Department of Defence bus to the Pentagon, prepared to spend the day there. I attended the U.S. Army Intelligence briefing, collected any documents which the Americans were prepared to release and which I felt might be of interest to the MI Directorate in London. All the British Officers in my detachment wore plain clothes and I would visit each of them in turn at their desks; I would then discuss any interesting development both with my staff officer and with his U.S. opposite number. I also made a particular point of keeping in close touch with the various U.S. Branch Chiefs – under whom my officers were working – and had lunch with each of them from time to time. I used these occasions to raise with the U.S. Branch Chiefs any difficulty or suggestion which had been raised in the course of my discussions. Later in the day I would return to my office with the documents and notes from my Pentagon visit and, every few days, would write to the Director of Military Intelligence describing what was going on.

Though I was a complete novice as regards intelligence I did find that, from time to time and increasingly, the U.S. branches seemed prepared to discuss particular matters. It was especially gratifying to me that they gradually appeared more willing – and were sometimes eager – to talk about the Middle East. This had, for a long time, been a virtually forbidden subject between our countries, made worse of course by the Suez Expedition which we had just carried out; indeed it was even worse than that since the Americans were well aware that I was the G.S.O.1 of the Corps that did it! To ensure that we encouraged this spirit of co-operation both I and my staff – and even more important, our wives, did a great deal of entertaining of the whole of the U.S. Army Intelligence Department. This not only contained many staff officers but also a large number of civilians. All, high and low alike, were important to us; questions constantly arose which made it necessary to approach a quite junior staff officer or civilian in some obscure corner of the building. Often this particular individual knew the background as no one else did – and he would view you with a good deal of suspicion unless he knew you.

Thus the entertaining became of paramount importance and all this fell on Pam's shoulders – and splendidly she did it. For much of the year we gave parties three or four times a week – some large and some small; and we went out frequently as well, so we were seldom in by ourselves. It would be hard to over-emphasise the help that this was to me in my work in the Pentagon.

Of course, one got to know and like some of the U.S. officers and officials better than others. One day a very good friend, a Colonel Neil asked me to dine with him (alone) at his club. During the meal he said 'You know you are in some trouble in the (Intelligence) Department – you are under suspicion of spying, and your future is being actively considered!' He went on to say that I had been seen around much more than had British Officers in the past. He emphasised that it was only because he considered me a good friend – and because he himself valued our countries' co-operation immensely – that he could speak so frankly; he had, he said, told his colleagues over and over again that we were both 'on the same side'. He explained to me that it had to be remembered that in general Americans could be divided into two groups – Anglophobes and Anglophiles; the latter were in a majority by far, but the Anglophobes were capable of making a great deal of trouble. He suggested that I lay low for a bit whilst all the discussion was taking place and he thought that it might well blow over completely – which I am glad to say it did; he was a helpful chap and it must have taken a lot of courage to warn me. The whole incident gave me a jolt, however.

In addition to my normal routine I had the duty of looking after visitors from London. Mostly these were from the MI Directorate and these I would take to the Pentagon and ensure they met all the people they planned to see. In the case of the DMI himself – a frequent visitor – the U.S. Chief of Army Intelligence would usually ask him to speak after the morning briefing, and would then give him lunch in the Pentagon where there were a number of small dining rooms for this purpose. We normally gave a party in our flat for the visiting officer. There was one very special, and from the British point of view very important, visitor – General Strong. He was head of our Joint Intelligence Bureau and he had been the President's (when he was Commander in Chief for the Normandy landings) Chief of Intelligence. Eisenhower was always greatly loyal to all who had served him well and, as with General Strong, insisted that they come and see him whenever they came to Washington. So, when General Strong came I would meet him at the airport and take him to the Pentagon as with the DMI; during the visit, however, there would always be an appointment with the President at the White House as well, to which I would escort him. From the little he was able to tell me of his conversations these sessions were most interesting; but what he had to say when he returned to England must have been very valuable indeed to the Foreign Office, as it was rare for us to have such a close and cordial link with our American Allies on that level.

Unfortunately I did not succeed in getting my office in the Pentagon. I felt, however, that I must have done something to pave the way as, just before Pam and I departed, after my three years were up, we were given a formal and most lavish lunch in Washington presided over by General Willems, the U.S. Army Chief of Intelligence himself. He made a speech which kept me blushing uneasily for about five minutes, and indicated that the U.S. authorities were coming round to the idea of my successor having a Pentagon office. As he sat down he presented Pam with an enormous bouquet and me with an engraved cigarette box. After lunch I was speaking to one of my best friends in the U.S. Department, a Colonel Bob Mulloy, and said how delighted and grateful I was; at the same time I drew attention to the period, only eighteen months earlier, when they almost had me out. I asked him what in particular had changed things. He just smiled and simply said, 'I'm afraid I can't say much; just that we had to be sure.' When I got back to England I found that General Willems had written to the Director of Military Intelligence about my tour of duty in the most – undeservedly – flattering terms. I learned two years later that my successor had indeed got the Pentagon office.

Whilst we were in the U.S.A. we had tried to travel as much as we possibly could. Fortunately I was given U.K. periods of leave together with U.S. rates of pay – an almost ideal combination. Soon after we had arrived in Washington we had bought a Buick car, which comfortably housed the four of us together with suitcases, a large ice box and – on occasions – fishing rods too. The weather in the summer is very hot throughout the United States, and the ice box was absolutely essential; everyone had them and blocks of ice to keep them cool were available wherever we went.

In March 1958, when we had been in Washington about nine months and had found our feet, we undertook our first long journey – to Florida. It was about a 2,500-miles-round trip, but a marvellous feeling leaving Washington in the very cold weather and, daily, getting warmer as we drove south. Every night we stayed in a motel; these are well advertised and cheap – often only four dollars a night in those days. The rooms were basically, but adequately, furnished with bed, chairs, a refrigerator and a TV set; we fed ourselves in our room from our ice box which we would re-fill at a supermarket every two or three days. There was always a coffee shop somewhere nearby, if food ran a bit short; and we could get a good breakfast there before starting in the morning. We spent a fortnight in Florida visiting the Everglades (a large and swampy area with all kinds of aquatic mammal and fish – and the means to get a good view of them), Key West (at the end of a long string of islands, connected by enormous bridges, which lead out to sea – to within ninety miles of Cuba) and other fascinating places. The climate was superbly warm whilst both Washington and New York were under snow. Before returning to Washington we spent a few days at Daytona with its spacious sands; this particular scene was only marred by the fact that the sand is also used by cars, the drivers of which seem to use it as a speed track, so it is not so peaceful as it might be. We returned to Washington refreshed – and sunburnt.

Later in 1958 we went to Eastern Canada, driving up through New England to Quebec. We spent two nights in Quebec City, in a motel; here we visited the Citadel and the Heights of Abraham where General Wolfe had won his famous victory over the French 200 years earlier. Every night the XXII Canadian Regiment beat Retreat at the Citadel – retiring to the tune of 'Auld Lang Syne' – and a very moving ceremony it is. In Quebec City I found it impossible to get an English language newspaper except the *Wall Street Journal* which, I discovered like our *Financial Times*, was well worth reading, having excellent news coverage. We then went to Ottawa, a pleasant but not exciting city. It was, however, permissible to walk into the House of Commons without any particular authorisation and to listen to the debate, which was interesting to us. We then drove to Algonquin Park, a large area of Northern Canada where there are numerous superb lakes for fishing and bathing; many Canadians have summer houses or log cabins there, and drive out at weekends from Montreal and Toronto.

For Christmas in 1958 we motored down the Mississippi River, past the Plantation Houses made famous by Frances Parkinson Keyes, to New Orleans and the Gulf of Mexico. We stopped at one of these houses on Christmas Eve to look around; the owners came out and met us and were most hospitable, insisting on our going in and showing us around. We spent quite a time being entertained in this house which was called 'San Francisco'; it was a pleasant and instructive interlude in our long journey to the

South. We spent Christmas Day in sunshine at a small town called Biloxi on the Gulf of Mexico; after this we went to New Orleans for a day or two and then returned to Washington.

It was, however, in the summer of 1959 that we did our longest, and most interesting, drive – to California – a round trip of over 9,000 miles. We took the route of the motorway through Pittsburgh and Chicago to the plains of Dakota, driving some 500 miles a day and, again, staying in motels; but, since it was very hot, we sometimes paid a bit more on this occasion and chose one with a swimming pool. After Dakota we struck north through Montana into the Canadian Rocky Mountains; Here we stayed in log cabins which were even more primitive than the cheapest of motels. The toilet arrangements were outside and very limited at the log cabin we had chosen near Banff. One evening, before going to bed, I wandered down the grass outside for some fifty yards – to attend to my needs; in the course of this I sensed something moving close behind me and, slowly turning my head around, I saw two colossal horns towering above me. There were a couple of moose which are, I believe, harmless animals; but they seem very large and threatening when you are close to them – especially if you are in pyjamas. I completed my business and returned to the cabin at the double. From the Rocky Mountains we drove through Washington State and down the coast of Oregon to San Francisco. The drive took us through the striking scenery of the Pacific coast and also through the Redwood forests of California with their enormous trees. In San Francisco – one of the most attractive of America's cities – we spent the best part of a week, before starting on the return trip.

It is very interesting for a foreigner to travel to the west of the U.S.; as you motor westwards you find that people know less and less about Europe, and they are vastly more concerned with the Pacific, Australia and the Far East. We were in fact frequently taken for Australians. All this can better be appreciated when one realises that there is no real national press as we know it; it is true that papers like the *New York Times* and the *Washington Post* can be found in the bigger cities, but in the main people read local papers. These reflect the thoughts of the people they serve and, in the west therefore, their coverage of foreign matters is mainly of the Pacific.

We drove through Nevada, stopping for a night at Reno; here – as at Las Vegas – they gamble throughout the twenty-four hours, mostly on fruit machines using silver dollars which are almost unobtainable in the Eastern States. One gets the impression in Nevada of very lax laws; the Marriage Registrar is about thirty yards from the Divorce Court – which about illustrates what life is like there. It is almost all desert and it is, I think, the only state which has no speed limit for cars. From Reno we went to Yellowstone Park with its fine scenery and famous geysers; we left Yellowstone just two days before a major earthquake, which was lucky. From here we went out of our way southwards to Wyoming as I had been asked to go to Caspar and collect a very old mitre cap. This was part of the uniform worn by the British infantry over 300 years ago; it had been presented to the newly-opened Army Museum in Chelsea by an American who had made a life-long study of British Army insignia through history. His drawing room was an amazing sight; the walls were covered by cap badges and other embellishments appertaining to almost every regiment in the British Army. I had not only to collect the cap, but to get it safely back to the Army Museum when I next went home for a meeting; it was a most fragile article and I found it far easier to collect than to ensure its safe travel.

We returned to Washington, after travelling for six weeks. It was quite the most interesting journey I had ever made, and I think my family felt the same. Certainly being in America these three years was a wonderful experience for all of us.

Chapter 17

A final tour of duty at the War Office

In July 1960 I returned to England to take command of the Driving and Maintenance School at Bovington Camp in Dorset. Here I was to work with many officers, warrant officers and N.C.O.s whom I had known well in the past. In particular Colonel (later Brigadier) Sir Frederick Coates, who was in command of a sister establishment known as the School of Tank Technology. I had known Freddy since we both joined the army almost at the same time; he had married when we were together in Cairo at the outbreak of war. He had lost a leg during the war but, despite this, was an amazingly active man; both he and his wife, Johnny, were dedicated and energetic yachtsmen and took part in many ocean-going races. They were with us in Washington and were superb hosts; this led to our getting to know many Americans we would not otherwise have met. They have been firm friends for many years.

I spent two very pleasant years in Dorset, and was then appointed once more to the War Office – this time as Assistant Adjutant General of the branch known as MP1; As in SD4, ten years earlier, this branch was concerned with manpower planning.

One of my responsibilities in connection with the officer intake was the Regular Commissions Board at Westbury in Wiltshire. Applicants for commissions – Regular or Short Service – had to pass this board; they would stay at Westbury for three days during which time they would have discussions and physical tests, so that the staff could look at their reaction to different situations and assess their leadership qualities. At the time I arrived in the War Office to take over my appointment it was becoming evident that too may candidates were being failed, on what can only be said to be grounds of prejudice. I felt that the R.C.B. certainly meant well; they had a paramount duty to keep high the standard of officer passing into the Army. The real trouble was that no attempt was being made to put 'round pegs into round holes'. Thus I wondered if it was really necessary for a candidate for the Royal Electrical and Mechanical Engineers (R.E.M.E.), who might be an excellent mechanic and who would spend most of his service concerned with vehicles – and perhaps eventually command a workshop – should need to show exceptional skill and speed in crossing a river on a rope? He clearly should have good powers of leadership, but would he really need the same physical prowess as, say, one destined for the infantry? I also felt that, important though these things may be, the ability to be a good member of the officers' mess did not solely depend on your accent. In this latter connection I could not help thinking of the superb wartime officers, promoted from the ranks, who settled into messes at the end of the war without the slightest difficulty.

After discussing all this with my director – the Director of Recruiting – I was sent to Westbury for a week to see if I could persuade them to modify their methods on the lines I suggested. I had long discussions with the Commandant and his staff; and I watched all the discussions and physical tests – and attended their summing up meetings to establish the grade of the candidates. In the course of this I found a number of anomalies; in particular there was a candidate for the Royal Army Ordnance Corps (R.A.O.C.) who did brilliantly in the discussions, showing all the required qualities, but failed a rope climbing test and did not pass. I assembled all my notes and, on my last day, again went to see the Commandant. I again emphasised that we were simply not getting enough officers into the Army to fill all our establishments; and I pointed to candidates who had failed and who might at least be given a second chance. However, it was of no avail; he simply said that his sole concern was that no officer should be commissioned unless he fitted in precisely with the picture of an acceptable officer as seen through the eyes of the R.C.B. So I returned to London in a state of some despair and discussed my fears for the future with my Director. The whole matter eventually went to the Army Council and – gradually – things began to change for the better, but it took some years.

One other event occurred about this time; it concerned the other part of my branch which was to ensure that each individual arm of the service had its correct number of men. In 1963 there was a mutiny in the Scots Guards who were on duty in London and who, at the time, were commanded by a Colonel Duffy. It had become pretty clear to us in the branch that the guard duties were far too much for this Regiment which was attempting to man two battalions – one at home and one overseas – whereas they could only recruit enough men for one; thus both battalions were seriously below strength. However, it seemed, from the reports we were getting, that it was also the case that the Commanding Officer was insufficiently aware of what was happening in his battalion. The incident got a lot of press publicity, and there was much interest from members of Parliament. One day when – as ill luck would have it – my General was away, I had a message from the Secretary of State for War (Mr. John Profumo) that he wished to see someone who knew about the situation in the Scots Guards. Since I was the most senior officer around concerned with manpower, I had to go – albeit reluctantly – to his office. I must say that the office itself was an education; it was all newly decorated in powder blue with a large photograph of his wife (Valerie Hobson) on his desk. The Adjutant General was present, together with a bevy of senior officers. When all were assembled Mr. Profumo turned to me and asked me to explain what had happened; when I finished he turned to the Adjutant General and said, 'What Pile has said is all very well, but I want the thing hushed up and I expect you to do it.' The amazing thing for me as I look back on this incident is less his (in my view unwise) dismissal of all the facts, but his utter coolness; the following day was the occasion he admitted lying to the House of Commons over his affair with Christine Keeler. This affair had in fact been going on for some months and, if at that time he was on tenterhooks as one would have expected, he certainly did not show it at our meeting.

After I had been at the War Office for a few months I took the advice of the Military Secretary as to what my likely future in the Army was. He told me that, in due course, I could get promoted to Brigadier on the staff; but that it was unlikely that I would get promoted in command as I had not completed my period in command of the Leeds Rifles. He acknowledged that this was in no way my fault, but said that only a very small proportion of officers who *had* completed their full time in command were getting promotion owing to the acute shortage of vacancies and that, in the light of this, I should not feel too sorry for myself. As a result of this conversation I thought that, rather than carrying on in the Army, increasingly bypassed by many officers now junior to me, it would be better to strike out anew, and get some experience of life in industry. So I set about looking for a suitable job; eventually I learned of a vacancy for a manager in Vaux and Associated Breweries in Sunderland. I decided to apply for this post, and went to see the Chairman, Mr. Douglas Nicholson. He told me, after the interview, that he would telephone me in London to let me know the result – but he gave me to understand that I would almost certainly get the job. So, on my return to London – and after a year in my appointment in M.P.1 – I wrote a letter resigning my commission.

Chapter 18

Vaux and Associated Breweries

In due course Mr. Douglas Nicholson telephoned me as he had promised, confirming that I had got the job; I was to be responsible for the transport and distribution department embracing not only the distribution of beer and other products but Mr. Nicholson's magnificent array of coaches which he showed regularly; I was also to be concerned with one or two other aspects of the administration of the Brewery. He proposed to give me a salary of just under £3,000 a year, a second pension, a car and (if I wanted it) a house. He said he expected me to start work in a fortnight; at this I heaved a sigh of relief that I had already taken a chance and given notice of my retirement to the Army authorities – otherwise my date of leaving might have been delayed while a successor was found. I had taken Pam up to Sunderland with me when I went for my interview, and, despite the rather dreary town that Sunderland was, she seemed anxious for me to take the job – so I confirmed to Mr. Nicholson that I would do so.

When I arrived to take up my duties I went, of course, first to the Chairman's office. He said very little; just words to the effect that I should go straight to my department, I should not listen to my predecessor ('He was rotten'), my budget would be £4,000 a week ('Try not to exceed this but, if you feel you must do so, come and see me first'). The whole thing seemed very reasonable and I welcomed the prospect of buckling down to make a success of it.

However, I soon learned that Mr. Nicholson was an impossible man to work for, and that everything in the Brewery had to be subordinated to his personal needs; these had to be satisfied immediately whatever the hour of day or, more often, of night and irrespective of the fact that one might well be engaged on pressing Brewery business at the time. He completely intruded into the personal life of his employees – all of them; indeed, he did not consider they were entitled to private lives. To make matters worse

86

Vanessa had become very ill with osteomyelitis whilst at school in Haslemere, and was in hospital in Guildford. Naturally Pam and I wanted to visit her as often as possible; eventually Pam stayed near Guildford alone during the midweek periods, and I joined her at weekends. After several days, during which time Vanessa appeared to get worse, she was transferred to the Atkinson Morley Hospital in Wimbledon where her trouble was correctly diagnosed; she then started to get much better and eventually was able to come and join us in Sunderland. It had, however, been an enormous worry to us both, and she missed a year of school because of her illness. It may seem out of character, but was nevertheless to his credit, that Mr. Nicholson was very fond of children. He showed me much concern and sympathy over Vanessa's illness. He frequently asked after her and, when she was transferred north to Sunderland Hospital, he made it clear to me that I could visit her whenever I wished – whether in office hours or not.

The job itself in Vaux Breweries was very interesting; the Company extended to Edinburgh (where we owned Ushers Brewery), Kendal in Westmorland and Morpeth near Newcastle. In addition there were numerous hotels (Swallow), retail outlets and of course a large chain of public houses. In all these areas I had the same responsibilities as in Sunderland so I had precious little spare time and, since I had no deputy, I saw little chance of ever getting away on leave. In the early stages this did not seem to matter; later on I found a means of doing this – but never for long periods.

We bought a house in Cleadon, nearby, and soon made many friends – both within the Brewery and outside it; the chairmen of Palmers (then the largest department store in Sunderland) and of British Ropes we got to know particularly well. Our circle was, however, a small one but, perhaps as a result, we all had a very happy social life together. In the brewery itself I gradually learned more of the problems of transporting and distributing large quantities of liquid – whether beer or anything else – economically. I also got to know well practically all the men both in Sunderland and in the subsidiary Breweries, and tried to help them with any problems that arose. There was in fact a Brewery Personnel Officer, but he was largely involved in dealing with trade union and legal matters, and could not travel about as I did. In addition to the personal side of my job I was concerned with the purchase of much expensive capital equipment of all kinds – vehicles (we operated some 130 cars and 250 lorries in Sunderland and Edinburgh alone), workshop equipment and machinery needed to maintain and paint the coaches; indeed, anything required by the Company except that needed for the actual brewing operation – this was dealt with by the Head Brewer. Altogether it was a job which, after a few weeks, I felt was well within my capacity and which I would enjoy.

Outside my responsibility – but very important to the Brewery – were the horses. These were used to draw some of the drays and the Chairman's coaches; they were a valuable advertisement for the Brewery. This department was run by an ex-gunner, Colonel Bill Froud; We saw much of Bill and his wife Pam, whilst we were in Sunderland. He had an even more difficult time than I did with Mr. Nicholson, as he had to ride with him every morning; but he stood it well and looked after the horses most efficiently.

After a bit I began to read more extensively about the complicated legal requirements with which we had to comply; it gradually dawned on me that all was not well in this regard. The rules were extremely strict – in particular the number of hours for which it is permissible for a man to drive a lorry without a break; detailed log sheets have by law to be maintained daily and these can be inspected by the Traffic Commissioners at any time and without notice. I used to see every one of these each evening before I left the office but, having learned the law on the subject, I began scrutinizing them more carefully. It soon became crystal clear that we were disregarding this flagrantly – and had been doing so for years (I had in my office records going back several years and there appeared to have seldom been a period when the law was not being broken). Increasingly cases appeared in the local press of firms being prosecuted for this type of offence, and I felt convinced that it would only be a matter of time before the Commissioners came to see us, when we would not have a leg to stand on. At least I thought that we ought to stop our current practice and obey the law from now on; so I issued the necessary orders.

During the next few days various important people in the Brewery came to see me for no apparent reason – the subject in every case, however, came round to my instructions on drivers' hours. The Chief Accountant said that our profits would suffer dreadfully; the Sales Manager that his sales would drop dramatically and even my own Chief Clerk (who always seemed to have a hot line to the Chairman himself) came and told me that I was simply asking for trouble if I did such stupid things. Inevitably the whole thing got to Mr. Nicholson in short time and he asked me to come and see him; I thought, in my innocence, that nothing but good would come of discussing it all openly with him. After all, he was a leading figure in Sunderland, Chairman of the Magistrates and a leading member of the Brewers' Society – he would surely not want a prosecution with all the scandal this would bring, whatever his senior staff were saying. How wrong I was! Indeed he did make all the right noises; 'Of course I do not want to disobey the law,' he said: but the following moment he was adding, 'but it is up to you to make sure that our profits are maintained.' I told him that the Chief Accountant had explained that there was bound to be a very small decrease in the short term, since we were currently in effect making money by disregarding the law. To this he replied 'rubbish' and he clearly was not going to admit that anything was wrong – 'It is up to you to keep us within the law, and to do so without detracting from the Firm's level of profits; and I'll tell you now that, if you can't do this, I shall get someone who can.'

I returned to my office perplexed, chastened and rather worried. I did not want to invite the sack, impossible though I considered the Chairman had been; I was, I felt, getting into the job rather well and, furthermore, we had just bought a house. I came eventually to a rather unsatisfactory compromise; I would ensure that every employee knew the law by putting up notices everywhere explaining it in simple language, and emphasising that it must be obeyed. If a man did break the law, however, I would overlook it. How weak and ineffective this compromise was can be appreciated when it is realised that the Brewery had a 'bonus' scheme which provided considerable financial rewards to those who did the most work; these were of course the biggest law-breakers!

Some weeks later I was, as I feared I would be, visited by a representative from the Traffic Commissioners, who spent two days going through our records in great detail. He pointed out to me what I already knew – that we had been in breach of the law for many years; and, in due course the Company was served with a summons. I got no word of advice, help or even comment from Nicholson; just a curt note telling me to get a solicitor and, when the case came up, attend court with the Company Secretary – and defend the Brewery. The hearing lasted two days during which the prosecution repeated our misdeeds, emphasising that they went back many years. I was called as a witness by our solicitor who could clearly find practically nothing to say in our defence; so he turned to the Magistrates and said, 'I ask you to look at Colonel Pile and the sort of man he is – can you imagine him knowingly stooping to something like this?' The Magistrates were, however, unimpressed by all this. The Chairman pointed out that we were a very rich firm and the offences were quite inexcusable; we were found guilty and he imposed on us a very large fine.

I reported the result to Mr. Nicholson and he simply said, 'All right, go and tell the Chief Accountant to get it paid.' I suppose it really was a small matter in business terms, and that I was too sensitive; but the whole case worried me a lot and I began to realise that I would not stay long with Vaux Breweries.

At the end of 1964 an incident occurred which led to my viewing the Company – and, in particular, the Chairman – in even worse light. At Christmas and the New Year any brewery is incredibly busy; extra men are taken on and considerable overtime worked – all of which, from the point of view of the employees, is extremely profitable. On 31st December I had my plans laid as usual, and every man earmarked for a specific job. In the event, on New Year's Eve, two men failed to appear – which of course threw out the arrangements; apart from anything else it made it necessary for us to make up for the lost time by employing extra men on New Year's Day, when the wage rates were even higher. When I saw them, and asked for an explanation, they had nothing to say; I strongly suspected that they had simply decided that it would be more fun to go to a party – and the Foreman confirmed to me that he, too, was sure that this was the case. So I suspended them both for two days as a punishment; this meant that they would lose two days' pay. We had, by this time, a fairly militant branch of the Transport and General Workers Union in the Brewery and, within an hour or so, a deputation from the Union came and saw me; they virtually gave me an ultimatum – rescind the punishment which they considered too severe or the whole Brewery would be called out on strike. I, of course, told them that I would do no such thing, pointing out that the two men deserved fully this punishment as they were in clear breach of their undertaking – voluntarily given – to work on New Year's Eve. I then went straight to Mr. Nicholson to acquaint him with the situation. He told me that he agreed with my action in suspending the men, but that he himself would see the Union representatives nevertheless. Later he told me that he had informed them that he would not accede to their demands.

On the following morning at about 7.00 a.m. I had a telephone call at home from the Brewery Foreman, saying that none of the employees were coming into work; and that a large picket was forming outside the entrance to the Brewery. I got into my car at once, and drove into Sunderland to see what was happening. Having parked my car I walked to the entrance where some of the pickets were standing about. Between the main entrance and my office was a walk of 100 yards in the open; this was lined on each side by men (whom I recognised as our employees and with whom I had thought I was on good terms) yelling all kinds of abuse in foul language – and waving objects such as broken bottles to threaten me, and indeed anyone else who tried to get into the building. I estimated that there were about 200 men in all, lining the road. So I walked slowly on, trying to ignore the taunts, threats and language but inwardly feeling anything but calm. Eventually I arrived at my office door and (thankfully) closed it behind me; it was without doubt the most unpleasant experience I had had since the war.

A few minutes later the Foreman came in and asked if I would see three representatives of the union, who were outside; I said that I would – and in they came. They were men I knew particularly well, and with whom I had often in the past discussed ways of improving conditions of work within the Brewery to (I always understood) our mutual satisfaction. They sat down, all looking very cheerful and, indeed, friendly; after a pause one of them said, 'Don't be too worried, Colonel, this is just part of the industrial game!' I explained that it was hardly a good game for the Brewery – on which their livelihood depended – to be losing an enormous sum daily because of their irresponsibility. They said that all I had to do was to rescind the suspension; the offenders had, the Union felt, already suffered one day's loss of pay (this was in fact the day of the strike when none of them would get paid anyway) and that they considered this sufficient punishment. I told them that it was no punishment whatever; the two men had defaulted on their word and I had no intention of modifying the punishment in any way. As soon as they departed I again went to see the Chairman and told him how things were. Again he agreed to see the Union representatives himself and, this time, to my intense dismay, he said he would do what they asked and revoke the punishment I had awarded.

I went away and considered the whole position carefully. I was already concerned at the constant telephone calls I was receiving from Mr. Nicholson whilst at home in the evenings – always demanding something which could not, by any stretch of the imagination, be considered to be Brewery business; this was also becoming very irritating to Pam, particularly as the calls were invariably acrimonious. Now I had been completely let down over the strike. So I made up my mind. I went to see Mr. Nicholson the following day, gave him three months' notice and said that I wished to leave the firm on the 1st April (1965).

For the first time since my initial interview with him the Chairman became almost pleasant, and he talked to me for about half an hour trying to persuade me to stay. He was always making threats to his employees, but he was known to hate change when the time came; I can only think that he did not want the expense of obtaining someone else, or the trouble of training them when they arrived. I was quite adamant; I had had enough, and so had my family.

The news of my intention to leave got back to the shop floor quickly and, when eventually I returned to my office, I was met by the three rogues who had caused me all the trouble over the strike. Their leader, smiling, said, 'All the men are at this moment signing a petition asking for you to stay here.' Doubtless they found me a soft touch and feared getting a manager who would chase them more! Anyway, when I said they could save themselves the trouble as I had no thought of changing my mind, he replied, 'We thought you might say that, but we hope that the signed petition will be at least a nice testimonial for you when you apply for another job.' They could be arrogant and maddening – but they had a pleasant side.

Even during the period of my notice, Mr. Nicholson never gave up his intrusion into my spare time; and I feel that I must give one further example of his behaviour as no one who had not seen it at first hand would ever believe what the atmosphere was like – there was no one on the staff who did not have a similar fund of stories. Towards the end of March the telephone rang at 10.00 p.m.; it was Mr. Nicholson who said, 'You know that the Grand National is tomorrow?' I said that I did; 'Well,' he said, 'I want to see it.' I paused, debating in my mind whether he wanted a car – or what on earth else he could want. 'Of course I don't want a car,' he bellowed down the phone; 'you know perfectly well I hunt on Saturdays.' I hadn't the slightest idea what he was after; it was the sort of guessing game he enjoyed playing on the staff. Eventually, after a few further curt comments, he said, 'Naturally I want a television set fixed up to take to the meet.' I pointed out the time and, in return, received another bellow, 'I'm well aware of the time, get on to the Chairman of Radio Rentals and tell him what I want.'

Radio Rentals were in York, and since any TV set would presumably take a good time to set up in the morning I saw little chance of its being ready for a meet at 10.00 a.m. In any case I could not see the Chairman of such a big firm putting himself out for such a purpose. However, I rang him up full of apologies and, to my utter amazement, he said 'For Mr. Nicholson I will certainly do it.' The following morning I went early into the office to see what was happening and, as I drove into Sunderland High Street at about 7.00 a.m., there were two police barriers – one at each end of the street, thus closing it to traffic – and, between them, two Land-Rovers; one had, on its bonnet, a large screen and the other a tall aerial. The set was being tuned in. When the operation was completed the High Street was again opened to traffic, and the two vehicles disappeared – presumably to join the hunt! What it all cost I never knew as this was my last week with the firm.

He always seemed to get his way; so, on this occasions, did I. I left.

Chapter 19

The Royal Soldiers' Daughters School

It is not easy to find a job when you are (as I was) fifty, with no reference from your previous employer and in an area far away from your old friends and potential contacts. I did not in fact ask Douglas Nicholson for a reference; he had, on a previous occasion, told me that he would never give a reference to anyone who left his employment voluntarily, so I felt I would merely get snubbed if I did. However, about a fortnight before I was due to leave the firm I had a telephone call from a General Dalton who was the Controller of the London Zoo. He had heard by some means that I was not all that contented in Vaux Breweries; he told me that it was not about the zoo that he wished to speak (I was a little sorry to hear that!) but about a rather obscure and run-down charity in which he was interested. He asked me if the job of building it up would have any appeal to me; I thought it might, so I went to London and had lunch with him at the Zoo, after which he took me to Hampstead to see it.

It was he said, an old Crimean War charity; at the time it was founded there were many charities for boys but virtually none for girls. This one, known as the Royal Soldiers' Daughters' School, had been started to benefit girl orphans of non-commissioned officers and soldiers; as there were now far fewer orphans the charity had to an extent outlived its objects, but it still had funds and a building, and General Dalton believed that its objects could be applied to the education of the daughters of today's soldiers, particularly those whose parents were badly off.

We walked round the place; it was a particularly severe Victorian building with bars on the windows and consisting of large drab rooms – in fact more like a workhouse than a school. I met the staff who seemed quite pleasant and very dedicated; I also met two other Governors, one of whom was a General Birks of my Regiment and whom I knew well. They all explained to me that they were anxious that the whole school should be re-built on

93

modern lines, and that every effort should be made to improve its rather
dreary image, the education and indeed the entire atmosphere of the
charity.

At the end of the afternoon they asked me if I was interested in taking
this on. They also explained that there had, hitherto, been a woman
secretary but that, if I agreed to take the job, they would regard me as a
general manager to oversee it, under the direction of the Governors. I was
also told that there was, and would continue to be, a warden and a special
house committee of women governors to deal with matters concerning the
welfare and supervision of the girls – so all this would, to my relief, be
outside my province. My function would clearly mainly be to achieve the
rebuilding of the school; and, since my sole staff seemed to be one secretary
possibly assisted by a part-time typist, it was going to be a lot of hard work.
However, I thought it might well be interesting, so I told them that I would
like to accept the appointment.

The R.S.D.S., though still called a school, could no longer teach regularly
owing to the age span of the girls – from five to nineteen; it simply was not
practicable to have the range of staff and equipment to do this properly. So
our function was to find them really good schools (many eventually went to
the Greycoat Hospital at Victoria) and to act as an educational hostel. The
homework was supervised and a wide range of extra-curricula interests
fostered; and, as they were with us at weekends, their wider education was
encouraged through visits to the theatre, ballet, art galleries and other such
places in London. Some of the children were orphans or very poor; others
were the daughters of regular soldiers and quite well off. It was much
appreciated by the latter as it gave these girls continuity of education despite
their parents' moves both at home and abroad. Thus we had two distinct
categories of children; we made it a point of principle that no one except the
Governors, the warden and myself ever knew which was which. This aspect
worked very well and it was an extremely happy establishment.

So I set about the job of rebuilding the place. After speaking to an
architect it was estimated that, to do this really well for 150 girls, it would
cost in the region of £250,000; since we had barely enough money from our
investments to meet our running costs it would all have to be raised from
scratch. There followed, for me, many months of hard work – mainly
financial – on the project.

We had in the meantime sold our house in Sunderland, and had moved to
Great Bardfield in Essex where we found an attractive farmhouse; unfortunately, living in Great Bardfield proved unsatisfactory. It was half an
hour to the nearest station and the journey to Hampstead took about one

and three quarter hours. What we had not anticipated was that my office hours would be so long; I seldom managed to leave the office before 7.00 p.m. and, by this time, the trains from Liverpool Street Station were infrequent. Thus, at this time of the evening the journey took even longer. So I arranged to convert a room in the school as a double room for Pam and myself. During the day she took the opportunity to see parts of London she had never seen before, paying many visits to the law courts and to the Royal Academy among other places; at weekends we returned to our home in Essex. Even this arrangement was not completely satisfactory; Vanessa was starting training in London and Fiona, who was then in Tel Aviv with the Foreign Office, was due to come home soon and would probably want to work in London. So we bought a mews cottage in St. John's Wood – and we went even less frequently to Essex.

After three months I managed to produce a plan for the reconstruction of the school, which I felt I could show the Governors. I proposed to sell off half our present two and a half acres of land, since I thought that one and a quarter acres would be ample for the new building – also bearing in mind that it would be modern and far less rambling. This would have an additional advantage, assuming we could postpone offering possession of the land on which stood the existing building, that we could continue to function where we were at present whilst the construction (which it was estimated would take at least two years) went ahead on the site of our large and rather ill-kept garden area. The remaining money needed I was trying to raise by appeals to the public – particularly in Hampstead – and from Army charities such as the Army Benevolent Fund and the Guild of St. Helena; the latter was a women's Army charity which seemed at the time to have funds available, but they would have to be persuaded that ours was a suitable cause and came within the scope of their work. Through our architect I was in touch with several big construction companies; in the event we sold the land to Central and District Properties Ltd. who eventually made us a firm offer of £125,000. They also agreed to defer taking possession until our building had been completed, as we had hoped. Gradually more money came rolling in and, by the end of my first year at the R.S.D.S., we had some £80,000 to add to the money from the land. I invested this and was able to augment it by making some £25,000 from interest on short-term deposits in the City. So we were clearly well on the way to raising the money we thought we would need, and I asked the Governors for formal authority to start the ball rolling. This they gave me and, after putting out tenders to a number of firms, we selected Y. J. Lovell to carry out the building; they contracted to do this for £225,000. Early in

1967 the contracts were signed and building work started shortly after.

During the two years or so it had taken to reach the stage of building work actually starting, the Warden and I had given a lot of thought to the inside of the new building; above all we wanted to get a degree of privacy for the girls which had been totally lacking in the old building. So we went to visit a number of other schools, including the Quaker School at Reading and the Masonic School at Rickmansworth, both of which had been strongly recommended to us. It was at the Quaker School that we found the best design for a schoolchild's bedroom either of us had ever seen, and we decided to copy it. The older children all had their own rooms, so there was no problem; but with the younger ones, who would be three in a room, we had especially made dressing tables, each with a tall side, which provided every girl with a 'cubicle' – as well as having space for all her personal possessions. There were five floors of dormitories – one for each age group; every floor had its own common and TV room. The building had a very large flat roof, and this we proposed to lay out as a garden for the staff; it had superlative views over London; looking southwards to St. Paul's Cathedral and the River Thames.

Having got the new building started I set about, with the co-operation of the Warden, getting the children into better schools. We already had some at the Greycoat Hospital, but too many were still at large comprehensive schools in Hampstead. As a result of a number of discussions with the Principal of the Greycoat Hospital and with an excellent all-girl school at Primrose Hill, we managed during the next two years to get every girl moved into one of these two schools; by the start of 1970 the whole 'tone' had visibly improved and we had the satisfaction of seeing our first two girls achieve university places. They were, I am glad to say, the forerunners of several others.

In 1968 we sold our house in Essex and bought one in Sedlescombe in Sussex. Our children continued to use the mews house in St. John's Wood but, when the new school building had been completed in 1970, there was much less work to do and I found I could well manage by travelling up to London daily from Sussex. However, after a year of this, I got bored with the job which, though pleasant in its way, now involved only administration, paying the staff and keeping the accounts. The challenge for me was over – by the summer of 1971 I would have served six years with the R.S.D.S. and I decided to ask the Chairman, General 'Splosh' Jones (he had succeeded General Dalton), to relieve me.

Chapter 20

Journalism, charity and village life

Thus, by 1971 I had retired properly – at least from paid employment. I started my new life by taking a course at the London School of Journalism; this lasted six months and, I am glad to say, I managed to pass. By the end of 1972 I had produced my first article – about mortgages, and why you should think hard about repaying them before you have to; I sent this to *Money Mail* (the *Daily Mail* weekly financial supplement) and had no reply or acknowledgement for some three months. Then, just as I had quite written off any prospect of its being accepted, a short letter came – together with a handsome cheque; the following Wednesday I looked at the paper and, to my amazement, saw that they had given me the whole back page, and had illustrated it for me too! I wrote under my Christian names – Frederick Devereux – so as not to attract too much attention locally, and thus possibly becoming an unofficial (and very inadequate) financial advisor to Sedlescombe village.

I wrote two further articles for this newspaper. One was on annuities, and the other on the means for elderly people to raise money on an owner-occupied house to supplement their income. These were also accepted and, again after an agonisingly long period, cheques came through the post. Soon after this I had a telephone call from the City Editor asking if I was prepared to write another; I pointed out my very limited qualification and he replied, 'Don't you worry, Mr. Devereux – our readers are pretty thick, and your articles just suit them!' These money articles, however, took a long time to write and involved much research, some of this in London, to ensure that the facts and figures were correct. Furthermore, there were other subjects I wanted to try and the *Money Mail* commitment could well become almost full-time; so, with some reluctance, I declined.

I wrote two articles on cricket. The first was a short life of Ranjitsinji, the great Indian cricketer who eventually became one of England's leading batsmen. I also produced one on the origins of the Hastings cricket ground where I discovered many documents and photographs lying on the floor of the pavilion of the Central ground, many covered in spilt beer and badly damaged. A few were quite priceless, dating from the mid-nineteenth century; they must have been amongst the earliest photographs ever taken. The Ranjitsinji article was accepted by a magazine called *The Cricketer* and the Hastings ground article by *Sussex Life*.

I also wrote an article for the *Kent Messenger* on the Military Canal and Romney Marsh. This involved the most interesting research; the Kent Water Board kindly allowed me to spend a day with them and showed me how the canal, built originally as a defence against Napoleon, had become virtually a reservoir collecting water from the hills behind, which otherwise would flood the marsh in wet weather. Similarly, in very dry weather water would be pumped out of the canal into the ditches of the marsh to ensure that it never quite dried out. This was achieved through a network of automatic pumping stations situated at intervals along the length of the canal. The drainage of the marsh in very wet weather was further assisted by a series of non-return valves in the sea wall along the coast. Because of this Romney Marsh has remained a very fertile area for grass and other crops; and it has been enabled to sustain enormous flocks of its famous sheep.

I wrote a good many other articles, mostly of lesser length, and also a short history of Sedlescombe which I published as a booklet; this I sold over many years in the Sedlescombe Village store in aid of the village sports clubs association of which I was the chairman.

In addition I felt that, having been an officer of the Order of St. John of Jerusalem for so long, I ought to do something to further their cause. I had been able to do some small things for them whilst I was in America, but nothing very much. So I wrote to them; they seemed grateful and asked me to take on the visiting of the ex-service war disabled in East Sussex. This I did, and I continued to do so for six years until they decided to amalgamate this work with that of the government department who were already working in this field. As a result of this reorganisation the St. John section was disbanded and its voluntary workers no longer needed.

Finally Pam and I had thrown ourselves – probably too deeply for our good – into village life. I ran the village Sports Association with her help, and I was on the Parish Council. Together we ran the local Conservative Branch for eleven years; subsequently I became, and remained for five years, the Rye and Bexhill constituency Deputy Chairman. In this capacity I came across many interesting people, in particular the Honorary Treasurer, Alistair Birrell, who had served in the Royal Navy during the war; he was an able treasurer and it was a great comfort to have him by my side when conducting the large – and all too frequently argumentative – meetings. He and his wife, Ann, have been good friends. The other person I much respected from my period in politics was Mr. H. W. (Harry) Payne; one of the difficult problems faced by any constituency is to find good candidates for the often thankless task of serving on local councils. Harry was one such candidate and, not only did he fight a robust campaign to win an election against a well-known opponent, but he proved a splendid representative on the County Council. Unfortunately he had to retire after an all too short period on the Council, due to ill health; he and his wife, Kit, have since left Sussex to live near their family in Stamford.

We also travelled. Having had, for so many years (since Germany in 1948), a love of fishing – and finding hotels both increasingly expensive and unattractive – we bought a rather lavish Mercedes motor caravan. This was an excellent vehicle; it was self-contained with a loo, shower and, indeed, a complete hot water system. We used it for all kinds of purposes apart from the fishing; we went to weddings in it and visited friends all over the country using the caravan as a base. We also used it extensively for travelling, spending many winter weeks each year (at incredibly low cost) in the South of France, Portugal, Spain or Greece. The most fascinating trip we ever made was to Lapland, via Finland. This took us about six weeks; we stayed sixty miles north of the Arctic Circle in midsummer and fished the beautiful lakes which abound in those parts. The Laps are a simple people, but a joy to be with. They are totally honest; if you go to a bank there is no need for a glass division between you and the teller with the money. Life is peaceful, even in traffic; in Rovaniemi, the capital and biggest town in Lapland, cars would frequently stop for you if you got in their way in the street – and the driver would smile and doff his cap to you. We were very sad to leave and always hoped to return there one day.

Incidentally, in all our extensive travelling in the caravan, we were fortunate to be assisted by another brother officer – Donald Chidson, O.B.E., M.C., who was the Director of the Caravan Club. Donald served in the Royal Tank Regiment during the war. His wife, Valerie, was also on the staff of the Caravan Club. Both were a great help to us and have been good friends.

By 1982 we felt that our attractive house in Sedlescombe was becoming too big and expensive for us – and that we should retire more completely. So we moved to Battle and bought the only house we could find anywhere in Sussex or Kent with enough space to house our caravan, without being in the 'stately home' class.

Chapter 21

Remarriage

In 1983 Pam died – quite suddenly, of a heart attack, soon after we had got established in our Battle home. After forty-three years of extremely happy marriage it was a grievous blow to me.

I lived on in Battle through 1983 and, in April 1984, remarried – Josephine Culverwell. Josephine lived nearby, in Dallington; she had been a widow for two years and had been a good friend of ours. Like Pam and myself she had been very involved in working for the Conservative Party; indeed, we met her when she stood for election to the local district council. At that time we spent six weeks in the early part of 1983 helping her with her election campaign.

Josephine, like me, has two daughters. Fortunately both families (and the grandchildren) got on well together from the start; we have both had the great joy of being able to treat the whole – enlarged – family as one.

Since 1984 I have had nine marvellously happy years with Josephine; and I believe that my two daughters feel an enormous affection for her. I am deeply grateful to her for this – and indeed for much else. Similarly I like to feel that her two daughters, Angela and Ursula, think, too, that notwithstanding my rapidly approaching dotage, I can also be of some help to them whenever they need it. I shall always try to be so.

Since our marriage we have lived first in Dallington and then in Cowbeech. Each year we have not only been to Scotland to fish for salmon but have also travelled widely. We have visited almost all the countries of Western Europe, Egypt (for a cruise up the river Nile), Morocco and cruised the Eastern Mediterranean to Sicily, Greece, Turkey and Jugoslavia. In 1989 we visited the Eastern United States and, in 1990, India. Furthermore, we have three times visited Abu Dhabi where Angela and her husband Anthony live; we have both enjoyed these visits immensely. I need hardly say that we hope to be able to travel more in the future, though our house in Cowbeech – Beadles – which stands in four and a half acres makes more demands on our time than was the case in the past.

I consider myself incredibly fortunate to have found myself another consort, so sweet and charming, who enjoys the same things as I do – and who will put up with me.

Chapter 22

Conclusion

Thus ends my account of the life of a perhaps too unambitious, but a contented, man.

There were many good times. I never regret having joined the Royal Tank Regiment though I was pressed, at one time, to transfer to a cavalry regiment – which was considered a more fashionable thing to do. This, however, never interested me; the Royal Tanks gave me marvellous opportunities. I went to war with a body of men whose courage and professionalism were unsurpassed anywhere; and, after the war, I had the satisfaction of seeing the 1st Royal Tanks become one of the best regiments in the Army. Before I retired I had spent twenty-eight years with the Regiment.

I was also particularly glad to have been able, in the Pentagon, to push the cause of our country one small step forward in the field in which I was working; and I was overjoyed that my family had the wonderful opportunity of seeing so much of America.

I am sorry I did not make a better job of Vaux Brewery; I would have liked to have stayed on there.

Because of the interest I developed in the management of money I have often been asked why I did not leave the Army and become a stockbroker. This did not appeal to me as I have always been far more interested in people than in money. Despite not achieving high rank in the Army, I have had more interesting appointments than many of those who did; and I hardly remember a year – whilst in the Army or after – when I was not able to help someone significantly. It is this, above all, which has given me the greatest satisfaction; this indeed is better than riches.

A SQUADRON OF TANKS IN THE ADVANCE IN N. W. EUROPE 1944/45

(i) BEFORE MAKING CONTACT WITH THE ENEMY

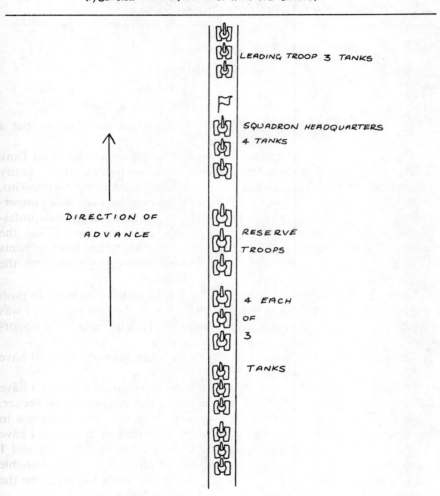

A SQUADRON OF TANKS IN THE ADVANCE IN NORTH WEST EUROPE 1944/45

(ii) AFTER MEETING A STRONG ENEMY DETACHMENT

ENEMY DETACHMENT FIRING DOWN THE ROAD HAS DISABLED OUR LEADING TANK

LEADING TANK IMMOBILISED

REMAINING TANKS OF LEADING TROOP DEPLOYED TO ENGAGE ENEMY FLANK

SQUADRON LEADER HAS JOINED TROOP LEADER TO SEE SITUATION FOR HIMSELF

R E S E R V E

T R O O P S

A SQUADRON OF TANKS IN THE ADVANCE IN NORTH WEST EUROPE 1944/45

(iii) DEPLOYED IN ATTACK

1ST TROOP STAYS IN POSITION
TO 'PIN' DOWN ENEMY WHILST
LEFT FLANK ATTACK PROCEEDS

SQUADRON LEADER LEADS
REMAINING TROOPS [12 TANKS]
TO POSITIONS FROM WHICH ENEMY
CAN BE ENGAGED FROM THE OTHER
FLANK

SQUADRON POSITION FOR THE NIGHT AFTER THE DAYS OPERATIONS HAVE BEEN CONCLUDED 1944 / 45

THE SITE — USUALLY A WOOD OR A VILLAGE — HAS TO BE DEFENDABLE AGAINST ENEMY ATTACK AND TO GIVE COVER FROM AERIAL DETECTION

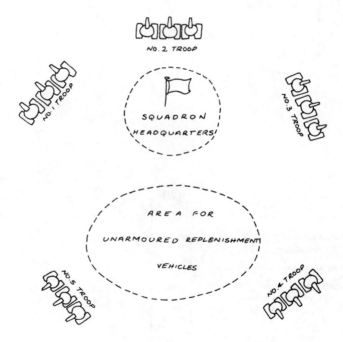

CAPTURE OF AHAUS AND HEEK MARCH 1945

NOT TO SCALE

(i) OUR ADVANCE HALTED

(ii) ADVANCE TO HEEK THE FOLLOWING DAY

HEEK

X REPORTED ENEMY GUNS

FARM BUILDINGS

↑ ROUTE OF ADVANCE

AHAUS

DENSE WOOD WITH ENEMY TANKS AND BAZOOKAS

TWO TANKS OF LEADING TROOP HIT AND SET ON FIRE

SQUADRON HEADQUARTERS

RESERVE TROOPS 12 TANKS

HEEK

X REPORTED ENEMY GUNS

AHAUS

DENSE WOOD WITH ENEMY TANKS AND BAZOOKAS

7 MILES

NOT TO SCALE

7 MILES